Indiscreet
MEMORIES

T0096257

Indiscreet

MEMORIES

1901 SINGAPORE THROUGH THE EYES OF
A COLONIAL ENGLISHMAN

EDWIN A. BROWN

monsoon

monsoonbooks

Published in 2007
by Monsoon Books Pte Ltd
52 Telok Blangah Road
#03-05 Telok Blangah House
Singapore 098829
www.monsoonbooks.com.sg

ISBN-13: 978-981-05-8691-1
ISBN-10: 981-05-8691-4

Copyright © Edwin A. Brown, 1935
First published by Kelly & Walsh, London 1935
The moral right of the author has been asserted.

All rights reserved. No part of this publication may be reproduced, stored in a retrieval system, or transmitted, in any form or by any means without the prior written permission of the publisher, nor be otherwise circulated in any form of binding or cover other than that in which it is published and without a similar condition being imposed on the subsequent purchaser.

Every effort has been made to contact the copyright holders of material reproduced in this text. In cases where these efforts have been unsuccessful, the copyright holders are asked to contact the publishers directly.

Cover photographs copyright © National Museum of Singapore, National Heritage Board.
Front cover photo: Sikh policemen, late nineteenth century.
Back cover photo: Malay postman, 1890 (GR Lambert & Co).

Printed in Singapore

12 11 10 09 08 07   1 2 3 4 5 6 7 8 9

Foreword

It may appear presumptuous on my part to add one more to the many volumes of memoirs that have been written by residents of the Straits Settlements and Malaya and possibly, when it is written, it will be of interest to no one but my own immediate relations.

When I first conceived the idea of this book and mentioned it to my family, one of my daughters remarked gravely that, though the idea was good in itself, she would hate to see me marked down on the station bookstalls from 17sh 6d to '2sh 6d to clear'.

Well, let us hope that such a disastrous ending will not come about. But even if it does, or even if this book is, in the end, considered worthy of public notice, it is not with that object alone that it is written, but so that my children, and perhaps succeeding generations of children, may learn something of the life in these parts, and of the East generally, at a time when Malaya was a very different place to live in from what it is now.

It is not my intention, in the following pages, to create anything like an accurate historical document of the day-by-day happenings in the times I write about. Rather it is to give, if possible, a picture of the everyday life of an ordinary, unconsidered member of the resident public, a picture that may be taken as an epitome of the average life of most of the people out here. There will be, I hope, no long dissertations on government policy, no dry-as-dust lists of statistics and figures, but rather a gathering together of incidents and stories of events, grave and gay, that have come directly into my life or into the lives of my friends during the early years of this century.

And of necessity, in a book of this kind, there must be mention made of many people. Most of them will have been friends, or at all events acquaintances, at one time or another. Many of them will be the principals in stories humorous or the reverse. In every case, if they read this book I hope they will realise that it is only for old times' sake that I make bold to use their names, and perhaps on occasions to poke a little fun at them or recount incidents of which they may possibly be the rather unfortunate centre.

And I feel sure that they are, if they are still alive, the same good sports today that they used to be then, and that they will allow me to make use of them in order to try and recapture some of the spirit of those good old days. Days which perhaps, after all, exist only in our imagination but which, nevertheless, go to make up a very pleasant dream.

There will, of necessity, be a frequent use of the personal pronoun. That must be excused because, in what is to all intents and purposes a narrative of personal doings, it cannot be helped. Other and perhaps fuller accounts of the happenings narrated in this book may be found elsewhere, notably in *A Hundred Years of Singapore*, written and published to commemorate the centenary of the Settlement of Singapore in 1919. The viewpoint taken in that book, however, was the viewpoint of the public as a whole.

Here, as I have said, you will find no general account of anything, but only the effect that that same event had on the mind of one individual, the eyewitness account, in fact.

And because I feel I may claim to have had some small hand in arranging many of the events referred to herein, and later on in fashioning in some small way the growth of what is now a great city, I ask the reader, or readers—for, as Hilaire Belloc says somewhere, it would be a pity if there were not more than one—to bear with me if at times that same personal pronoun referred to seems to be a little too much in evidence.

EDWIN A. BROWN
Singapore, 24 April 1934

1

1901

I arrived in Singapore on Friday, 4 January 1901. Of my voyage out and my preparations for coming out, it is unnecessary to speak; they were an experience which is gone through by all who come out today. The boats travelled on, or most of them, were quite as up to date then as now, the ports touched at were the same, the Red Sea was just as hot and the Suez Canal looked just as sandy. Everyone travelling to the East has, I feel, exactly the same experiences today as then, so that it will suffice if I say, as I said in my opening sentence, that 'I arrived'.

And I arrived at about ten o'clock at night on the SS *Hamburg* of the North German Lloyd.

I can remember to this day the lovely effect of the full moon on the entrance to the harbour and on the Pasir Panjang coastline. I can also remember seeing the German flag flying proudly from the top of one of the houses—I rather think that the house in question is, or stood on the spot, where the manager of the Harbour Board lives today. The residence in question was one occupied by a German mess, one of the members of which was the afterwards notorious Mr Diehn. Shortly after I arrived the *Singapore Free Press* waxed wroth in a leader upon the fact that

11

the visitor to Singapore saw the German flag first, and the mess were prevented from flying it any longer.

But I digress—

As the ship came alongside the old Borneo Wharf (now known as West Wharf) it started to rain, and went on doing so all the time I was transferring myself and my baggage to the gharries which Percy Cunliffe, who came down to meet me, had engaged.

I could see nothing of the roads over which I drove as the rain obscured everything, but I landed eventually and late at night at old Cluny House where Cunliffe was living with Begg (of Guthrie & Co.), McKean (of Paterson Simons, afterwards of Fraser & Neave) and a lawyer whose name I think was Laurie.

My first impressions of Singapore were of the colour green. Everything was green. Green grass, green trees, green undergrowth, green hedges—a wonderful vivid green. After the sand of the desert and the dust of Colombo, this green of the Malay Peninsula still enchants me.

I took a walk in the early hours of the morning of the day after my arrival along Cluny Road and into the gardens, and saw my first wild monkeys! I was thrilled.

The prettiest part of the town in those days was, of course, the esplanade. The road by the sea, now called Connaught Drive, was then bordered on both sides by magnificent old sturdy trees that had grown very tall. They were of so luxuriant a foliage that there was a definite roof of greenery the whole way along the road. In the evening both sides of the drive were full of stationary carriages, the lady occupants of which would walk about or sit in each other's carriages and chat, while their husbands played their games on the padang or discussed 'business' in the Singapore Club or the Cricket Club.

I remember being struck, even then, by the cleanliness of everything. The natives, mostly Chinese, looked clean and tidy in their white suits with baggy white or light blue silk trousers, the coats of the Chinese fastened with little braided buttons and the inevitable queue tucked into a hip pocket. It is interesting here to remember that it was not until the Chinese Revolution under Sun Yat-sen that the queue—or *towchang* to give it its proper name— was definitely discarded. Even the Straits-born Chinese followed the old custom in the matter of hair. When the Chinese company of Volunteers was formed, the men would fasten the *towchang* into the band of their hats and so keep it safely tucked away. They could not, however, take their hats off without disarranging their 'coiffure' and therefore, on the King's birthday parades when the command of 'Three cheers for the King' came, they were permitted to keep their hats on!

On the other side of the esplanade, now St Andrew's Road, the trees were flowering ones, with flame-of-the-forest and other lovely trees predominating. There have been times when we have driven along in our rickshaws to the office over a veritable carpet of yellow and red flowers. A very beautiful sight.

Another thing that left a great impression upon me at the time was the intense wetness. I arrived, of course, at the real rainy season—that is to say, the season when there was more rain than usual—and really everything was very damp with clothes, boots and shoes mildewed in a night. It was almost an impossibility to keep things in good order. Later on, when the jungle was cleared for rubber and the undergrowth done away with, climatic conditions improved a lot, but at the time I am writing of there was still heavy jungle over a large portion of the island and patches quite near the inhabited parts. General dampness was the rule.

The great majority of the native houses and shops were colourwashed a bluish white; red brick was quite an isolated sight and a large number of houses and nearly all the houses in the suburbs were roofed with attap thatch. Tiles, if used, were of Chinese make and not flat but rounded like a drainpipe cut down the centre. They were laid in rows alternately convex and concave, and gave a wavy look to the roofs which was quite nice to look at.

Roads were narrow, in many places only wide enough for two bullock carts to pass with difficulty, and with the sole exception of the esplanade there was not a footpath in the town. There were the five-foot ways, of course, in the business quarter, but as these were regularly used for the storage of goods they were not of much use to pedestrians.

Vehicular traffic consisted of the bullock cart and the hand-drawn cart for business purposes, and the rickshaw and horse and gig, horse and victoria, and pony and gharry for passenger traffic. Horse-drawn drays were scarce as a horse could only do a certain number of miles—and very few—per day, so it was not much use for business purposes, though John Little and Robinsons did their Tanglin delivery by horse and van.

A great deal of riding took place; the soft laterite roads were particularly suitable for this kind of recreation while roads like Holland Road, Ayer Rajah Road, Buena Vista Road, etc. were not even metalled, and were splendid places for a good gallop.

Tanjong Katong, of course, was 'the seaside'. One took a house and went down there to stay for two or three weeks to get a change of scenery. To go out and back in a day was almost more than a horse could manage after having done the usual journey into the office!

The firm I came out to join was Brinkmann and Company, the Singapore house of Hiltermann Bros. of Manchester. With the exception of Cunliffe, who had been out about two years, I was the only Englishman in the firm, the remainder being Germans. As time went on, more and more Englishmen were sent out from Manchester and before the Great War the German element had been practically eliminated.

It was the custom in those days for a new assistant to be taken round to the other firms and introduced to the various managers. It is a custom that disappeared some time ago, probably because the place got too large and people did not know each other so well, but it has always seemed to me, as it did at the time, to be a very friendly beginning to the life of a newly arrived young man.

I was duly escorted round the different firms and met then, for the first time, men who, in many cases, I was to know well in the future. It is interesting to remember that in the week I arrived four men who were later to become eminent and well known, for various reasons, were admitted to a partnership in their respective firms. W. Ewald to Huttenbach Bros.; James Graham to Syme and Co.; Hans Becker to Behn, Meyer & Co.; and John Saloman to Kumpers & Co. Poor old John Saloman! If ever a man suffered the slings and arrows of outrageous fortune it was he. Head of a snug business he was a German who had, in his day, spoken openly in Hamburg against what he saw. Feeling it would eventually lead his country to ruin, he lived to see everything he knew and loved disappear.

He was suspected here, quite unfairly, of being a secret service agent because he had been decorated by the Kaiser with some minor order. As a matter of pure fact he got the order because, out of the kindness of a great heart, he had paid for the upkeep and repair of the graves of German sailors who had died out here.

I brought him down from Kuala Lumpur where he had been interned during the 1915 Singapore Mutiny, and had perhaps some small hand in persuading the powers that be to allow him to live on in peace here instead of being sent with the other internees to Australia. He was given a small house in Tanglin Barracks and there he remained on parole with his wife until the end of the war, watching his property and possessions disappear, shunned by people who had called him friend, a broken-hearted man. There must have been many Germans like him scattered about the world who had seen the ruin that was to come to their country long before the fatal outbreak of war in 1914.

The air in January 1901 was full of rumours about a new governor. Sir Alexander Swettenham (the elder brother of Sir Frank) was 'acting' and was due to go, and a gentleman named Sir

Arthur Havelock was said to be coming to take his place. Another rumour placed Sir Frank Swettenham as the likely candidate. In due course Sir Frank was to step into his brother's shoes.

It is interesting to note that on Sunday, 6 January the Volunteers attended a parade at the Presbyterian Church where a mural tablet was unveiled to the memory of William Cloke, Sergeant SVA, who had thrown up his position in Singapore and gone to South Africa to join Thorneycroft's Mounted Infantry and take part in the Second Boer War. He died in Ladysmith in May 1900. He was the forerunner of many a gallant fellow who was to do the same some fourteen years later. May their example never be lost sight of.

I was left alone that morning, I remember, while Cunliffe and his fellow messmates attended the parade. I am not sure but I think the corps had its photograph taken outside the old town hall after the service was over.

My first days in the business life of Singapore were attended by drama. The first work that was given to me was stocktaking. It was a job that evidently was thoroughly disliked, and had obviously been left over for my arrival!

In those days the firms dealing in imports lived over their godowns. Collyer Quay was one long stretch of offices on the first floor (the only floor) of the buildings—the ground floor was taken up by the stores.

Having done stocktaking in a Manchester warehouse, I thought I knew all about the game and prepared to do it in my own way—a way obviously different from what the staff was accustomed to, as the sequel will show.

I spent a perspiring day in the dirt and dark—for in those stores there was very little daylight and certainly no artificial light—and at the end of the day brought the result up to the office, quite proud of myself, only to be informed that I was forty bales of grey supers out in my reckoning.

The manager of the Import Department obviously did not think much of his new assistant, and I was sent down to stocktake again. Another perspiring dirty day, with eyes open to make no mistake this time, but alas the result was the same. The matter was now looked upon as serious, and I was haled before the Tuan Besar who gave me a wigging, a lecture on carelessness and a threat that if I didn't get proper results next time I might have to be sent home as incompetent! And so, with my tail between my legs, I made fresh arrangements to do the stocktaking.

On arriving at the godown early next day, ready to get down to it, I was greeted by an excited crowd of coolies and assistant storekeepers, jabbering to me in Malay (which I didn't understand). But I soon found out the reason for there, on the floor of his office, lay the old storekeeper, dead! He had arrived before me and, hearing that I was to do the stocktaking again and realising that the game was up, had taken poison and killed himself.

So I had been right after all; the forty bales of grey supers were in the books all right but they weren't in the store! How long the swindle had been going on I never found out, or have forgotten if I did know, but I have always wondered *how* the assistants did the stocktaking in the days before I arrived! I suspect they took a good deal for granted!

I had, by this time, settled myself into Singapore and had taken a room at the Hotel de la Paix, the building of which is still standing in Coleman Street. At the time I refer to and for many years after, this hotel was a favourite one for residents. It was kept by an old lady called Mrs Kahlke, a widow of a sea captain, and she ran the place with due continental regard to cleanliness and good food. It was considered an honour to be asked by the old lady to come and have tea with herself and her two daughters in her parlour, and one had to be on one's very best behaviour all the time!

Both the girls were married later, and most of the old residents of the hotel attended their weddings.

I was, by this time, beginning to make friends, and was receiving invitations to dine at the houses of the Tuan Besars to whom I had been introduced. I had, of course, been taken round to put cards in the boxes of the wives of the gentlemen in question—this had to be done within a day or so of the introductions—and the invitations came along in due course. It was sometimes difficult to find one's way in the dark to a house that had only been seen once in the daytime, but I do not think I ever really lost my way. However, I couldn't speak to the gharry-wallah and none of them ever knew the names of roads or of houses, or of the people who lived in them!

Some were, however, less fortunate than I. A good story was doing the rounds when I arrived of a certain Swiss, newly arrived, who was taken round and duly received his invitation to dine the next Saturday at the house of Mr Sohst, a partner in a firm called Puttfarcken & Co. He set off in a gharry from the Adelphi Hotel, confident that he would be able to find his way.

On Monday morning the manager of Rautenberg, Schmidt & Co., in which firm he was, received a sarcastic chit from Mr Sohst suggesting that he should teach his newly joined assistants that when they were invited to dinner it was customary, in Singapore at all events, to turn up or to send a valid excuse!

The victim was sent for and confronted a very irate Tuan Besar. 'But I went, sir!' said the poor youth. 'I really did, and had an excellent evening, and thoroughly enjoyed myself, and I've been asked to go again as often as I like!'

Mr Sohst was rung up, but he insisted that his complaint was founded on fact.

So enquiries were made and it was found that the lad had set out from the Adelphi Hotel all right, but had completely lost his sense of direction in the dark, and instead of going to Mount Elizabeth had eventually fetched up at a well-lit house down at Keppel Harbour! A party was in progress, he was welcomed effusively by a cheery gentleman who expressed himself as very glad to see him, was quickly made to feel at home and, being a good pianist, was soon the centre of a very jovial evening. It was discovered afterwards that the house belonged to a pilot, who had never seen his guest before but thought that possibly he was someone who had been told to call on him!

Another story about the same man is founded on the fact that it was a habit among the youth of the place to pull the legs of newcomers about calling on the governor. All sorts of rules and regulations were made up on the spur of the moment to suit the gullibility of the greenhorn, and men have been sent up to call in the afternoon in full evening dress with brown boots and other weird sartorial effects too numerous to mention.

The story in question is as follows: This Swiss youth was told to go up and call. It was pointed out to him that he would find at the door a man in white clothes and a red hat who would try and persuade him to sign his name in a book. He was instructed to pay no attention to him. His advisers informed him that it was the pleasant habit of the governors to try and save themselves trouble by this method, and that only 'passers through' and people not sufficiently educated to do the polite thing fell for it. But the real gents, the men who knew what was what, always demanded to see the governor in order to hand him their card personally.

So away went our Swiss to Government House, fully determined to do the right thing. Everything fell out exactly as had been foretold. The man in white clothes and red hat, the book, the request to sign one's name, all were present and correct. But they couldn't fool our man! Oh no, he had come to call on the governor in the correct manner and he was going to do so.

While the argument in the hall was proceeding a gentleman came down the stairs and, noticing the altercation, came up and asked if he could be of any assistance. So our Swiss opened his heart to him and told him what he was there for, how he wanted to do the right thing and how the servant was trying to prevent him from doing it.

'You are quite right,' said Sir Charles Mitchell—for it was he—'I am the governor. Give me your card and come along upstairs and have some tea!' And the story goes that he took him all over the house, showed him the view from the tower and sent him away happy without ever letting the lad have an inkling that he had been the victim of a practical joke.

And when, next morning, the jokers asked him how he had got on at Government House, they found that the laugh had been turned against themselves!

On Saturday, 19 January Her Majesty the Queen was reported by Reuter to be unwell, and it was stated that physicians had been summoned to Osborne.

On Monday, 21 the telegrams reported grave anxiety, and later the summoning of the members of the royal family to Osborne.

Tuesday, 22 gave a ray of hope as a slight rally had occurred on the day before and a little food had been taken and some sleep. But it was only the final flicker of life, and the end came that same night.

On the Wednesday morning we knew that the Queen, our great Victoria, was dead!

I can remember even now, and shall never forget, the arrival of that news. It was as if the heart of the great British Empire had stopped beating. Something had happened that seemed to be beyond the power of human intelligence to grasp. Men looked at each other and said nothing, but the expression on all faces was the same. 'What is going to happen? To us? To the Empire? How can the world go on?' One had got so used to the fact that Queen Victoria ruled. No one out here could remember any other ruler, people had got to think of her as something fixed and unalterable, a necessity without which the Empire could not live.

The feelings at home at this sad time have been beautifully portrayed by Noel Coward in his great masterpiece, *Cavalcade*. It is not for me to attempt to add to that wonderful epic, but merely to try and show that the feelings that moved London at that time were moving the people of Malaya, as they were moving the whole of the British Empire.

I think the greatest tribute that can be paid to the memory of that great empress, and to the grief and sorrow that moved the world at that time, is to point to the fact that youngsters of the present day, seeing *Cavalcade* on the stage or film, simply do not understand that scene. It is beyond them. It is, in simple fact, beyond anyone who had not arrived at man's estate before it happened, and who experienced it personally in all its tragedy and solemnity.

On Saturday, 4 February the memorial service for the great sovereign was held in St Andrew's Cathedral. The time had been postponed until a quarter past six in the evening to coincide with the time of the funeral at Windsor. I suppose that never before had such an awe-inspiring service been held there, and possibly it has only been equalled once since, namely at the Armistice Service in November 1918.

It had been a dull, sunless day, making everyone conscious of the deep sense of awe and depression that was holding the Empire in bondage at the time. The attendance at the service overflowed the cathedral, filled the porches and a large portion of the roads round the building.

The service was taken by Bishop Hose, assisted by Archdeacon Perham and the Revs. Gomez and Stubbs. When the chancel was reached the psalms thirty-nine and ninety were sung, these being followed by the lesson, taken from I Corinthians XV.

Then came the hymn, 'Now the labourer's task is o'er', followed by the burial service. The service concluded with an anthem selected and adapted specially by Mr C.B. Buckley, the choirmaster, introducing a trio by Sir Frederick Ouseley and parts of a creed by Vincent Novello, the appropriate words being taken from the books of Wisdom and Ecclesiasticus. (This anthem is still in the choir library of the cathedral.)

Thus ended a service, 'the likes of which,' said the *Singapore Free Press* at the time, 'St Andrew's Cathedral will hardly ever again witness.'

It was calculated that, including those in the porches and in the grounds, from 1,400 to 1,500 people must have been present and certainly, if that estimate was correct, there never has been such an attendance at any service up to the present day.

And I am in a position to know, for the next week I joined the choir and have been a member of that body ever since. I had been unable to get into the cathedral for the service, and had to be content with a place in the crowd outside the West Porch. But I shall never forget the reverence and the solemn attitude of that crowd, many of whom, from their position, could see nothing at all and hear very little but the singing of the hymns.

An interesting sidelight on the reverence and respect in which all nationalities held the late empress is shown by the following paragraph in the *Singapore Free Press* of the day:

'The appearance of the town of Singapore was remarkable ... Those who went through the native parts of the city on Saturday saw a perfectly silent town, as far as business went. So literally were the orders of the heads of the various communities to stop business being carried out that bakers, in many instances, ceased to make bread and the food shops were shut up. Even the rickshaw coolies and bullock-cart drivers refused at first to go on the streets, as they said it would be *salah* ... But for the crowds of people going quietly about the streets, it seemed like a city struck with the plague.'

So much for the death and funeral of the great Queen. It is a period of my life that I shall never forget. I have seen monarchs come and monarchs go since that day, but the thrill and the solemnity of that time is still with me and will, I expect, remain.

To turn to lighter matters. About this time it was proposed to form a Volunteer and public band. Public support was to be called for, and the band was to act as a town band and to be at the service of the Volunteers when required.

It was duly formed, but I remember little about its public performances, never having heard one to my knowledge. But I had one vivid experience of it, and the story can be read in the reminiscences of old-day volunteering which I wrote many years afterwards for the *Singapore Free Press* entitled 'The Bad Old

Days'.

Tigers were still on the island in those early days of my residence here, and it was not a very unusual occurrence for them to be seen. Men of the 16th Madras Light Infantry, out Changi way for field firing at the end of January, were startled by one crossing the road in front of them.

Changi and the district around had always been a haunt for tigers. It was said that the females of the species would swim over from Johore to Pulau Ubin, take a 'breather' there and then complete the journey to the island, landing at Fairy Point, and give birth to their young in that neighbourhood. Almost up to the time of the first occupation of Changi by the military, the remains of the old tiger pits, mentioned by Buckley, could still be seen on the high ground back from the coastline.

The tigers seen on the island were generally young ones, not fully grown. It would appear that they swam back to Johore as soon as they were big enough and strong enough to essay the journey.

A little incident occurred on 21 January of this year which will be of interest to members of the cathedral congregation and to the staff.

The Rev. Stubbs and Lionel Koek (a member of the choir) were passing the cathedral in rickshaws when they saw a light in the tower. Taking the lamps from their vehicles they started off to investigate. At the foot of the spiral stairs they called out, 'Who's there?' and the lights went out. Up they went, warily, to discover a Chinese bell-ringer and two German or Dutch beachcombers.

All were later fined for trespassing, but it appeared that the bell-ringer, with true Oriental opportunism, had been in the habit of turning an honest (?) cent or two by letting out the belfry as a dosshouse.

Another tiger was reported on 13 February, and this time was hunted by Messrs Maw and Heytman. Maw, the owner of Motion & Co., nautical instrument makers and opticians, was a great *shikari*, and he and Mr G.P. Owen were generally the first out after any big game was reported on the island. A little bit of a doggerel made up about the two of them has stuck in my memory. It was probably quite libellous as regards their financial position, but was clever:

> 'Owen and Maw went out one day
> Owen Maw than they could pay.
> Owen and Maw came back they say
> Owen Maw.'

A bicycle club existed in Singapore in 1901. I was never a member. I was never an enthusiastic cyclist—probably because I was such a bad rider—but for a time it was a flourishing club. The last remaining member of it disappeared from Singapore when Walter Makepeace retired a few years ago. I knew many of the members—St Clair, Lanz, Laugher (a master at Raffles who played the clarinet every evening after dinner as a recreation)—and was often asked to join, but did not do so. The club used to go on cycling picnics, getting at times as far away from the town as Bedok and the Thompson Road Reservoir! If they rode to Changi it was a red-letter day, and could only be done on a whole holiday.

I had left the Hotel de la Paix after about a month, and gone to live with a Mr and Mrs Whitefield who kept a boarding house at Zetland House in Armenian Street. Looking at that house today people will laugh when I say that it was, at that time, one of the 'posh' boarding houses of the town. Whitefield was then the manager of the Robinson Piano Company and the hon. pianist of the Philharmonic Society, besides being a very good fellow and always ready to oblige with his musical talent. Mrs Whitefield was an excellent housekeeper and kept a splendid table. It is not to be wondered at, therefore, that she attracted to her house many of the young men who were afterwards to rise to importance in the town and elsewhere. A.B. Cross, a lawyer and a wonderful musician himself, was there. Billings, afterwards Head of the Shanghai Public School, was also one of us. Three Whites—H.T., afterwards managing director of Robinsons, 'Windy' (or W.A.), a Canadian in the Sun Life of Canada and 'Capt.', the head of the Tanjong Pagar Lighterage Department—lived there too. Others were Nellis of Standard Oil, 'Wullie' Goldie of McAlister, who retired some time ago, and others. George Penny used to be a frequent visitor, especially when we got up variety entertainments, as we did frequently. Ambrose Cross used to write small plays for us, and we would perform them in the long drawing room. I wonder if the Rt Hon. Sir George Penny, Bart., MP, ever remembers the wonderful show he put up in the first performance of *Blood for Blood* or *Why She Did It*, played in that long room at Zetland House. It was a great show and convulsed the audience, I remember.

At Zetland House I met the great Bertram, probably the greatest conjurer of all time. I met Mr Sydney Brough and his wife (I am not sure, but I think that same Mrs Brough is the Mary who was, for a long time, with Walls and Lynn in the Aldwych farces and is now taking part in the film productions of those plays) and a host of other interesting professional people who passed through Singapore.

They used to come up to dinner with the Whitefields before the shows, and then all of us used to troop down to the old town hall to see their performance.

2

1901 (Continued)

On Monday, 11 March the first advertisements appeared in the papers of the coming performances of *At Zero*, a musical romance in three acts, the music by Frederick Rosse and the words by Lester Teale. It was common knowledge that under this latter name was concealed the identity of Captain H.T. Wynter of the RA, the producer of the play.

As this was the first show I ever took part in in Singapore, some account of it and of the methods of producing shows in those days may be interesting.

At the time of my first appearance on the stage in Singapore, amateur dramatic effort was distinctly a private affair, and was the result of some special enthusiasm on the part of one individual. There was no committee and no society. The method of procedure was something like this: 'Let us,' said the enthusiast, 'get up a show.' If a sufficient number of people agreed then certain influential men in the place were interviewed and asked to become guarantors at S$100 or so per head. When S$1,000 had been obtained in this way, rehearsals commenced and in due course the public performances were given.

I believe I am right in saying that it was very seldom that

a profit was made, and the guarantors nearly always lost their money; but as they seemed to have the right to come along to all rehearsals and onto the stage during performances, and imbibe drinks with the cast (drinks were always free during rehearsals as well as throughout the run), I have no doubt that they got their money's worth.

I have no doubt also that the custom of free drinks to all performers had a good deal to do with the lack of profit when the balance sheet came to be drawn up.

The theatre itself—it was called a theatre because it had a stage—was a funny affair.

Every time a show came to town the papers bewailed the lack of facilities. It was situated in the bottom room of the town hall, a building which stood on the site of the present Victoria Theatre. Indeed the upright pillars at the sides of the present auditorium are the actual pillars that held up the concert room on the first floor of the previous town hall.

The possibilities of the stage were limited. There were no 'flies'. The ceiling was the same as that of the hall. The top of the proscenium was only about two feet from the ceiling so that in setting a stage, borders had to be fastened to the rafters and never properly masked, except from the well back in the pit.

There were two dressing rooms, one on either side, and that was all. One stepped out from the dressing rooms almost into the view of the audience sitting in the side seats.

Lighting arrangements consisted of gas footlights and three rows of gas borders, all controlled from the same tap. When the tap was horizontal there was a blackout, when vertical, lights were fully on and, to paraphrase the case of the noble Duke of York, 'when it was halfway up, they were neither up nor down'. And these were all the lighting effects obtainable.

The stage was about two feet off the ground, and a hole about a foot deep had been hollowed out in front of it to make a place for an orchestra.

It will be understood from these preliminary remarks that the production of stage plays was carried out under somewhat difficult conditions. When to the above is added the fact that the auditorium was lit by gas, that there were no *punkah*s and that stage and dressing rooms had a temperature popularly supposed to belong only to the nether regions, some idea of the triumph of mind over matter in dramatic affairs can be gathered.

I was in the Cricket Club one evening when a man called Tonkin came up and spoke to me. Tonkin was an assistant in the firm of Arthur Barker & Co., in which firm also was H.W. Noon and a man called Kirk, one of the best tenors that Singapore has had in my lifetime. I asked Tonkin where he was going and he said, 'To rehearsal.' He mentioned that a play called *At Zero* was being produced, and asked me if I was interested in that sort of thing. I didn't wish to say too much, having no idea whatever of the standard of dramatics out here, so I contented myself with saying that I had done a bit of it and would like to do some more. He said, 'Why not come along now? We want some more men in the chorus.' So I agreed and we walked over to the old town hall.

I can remember to this day the shock I got when I saw the antediluvian arrangements of the stage, but sensed immediately that I was in for some fun, so kept my mouth shut while I was being introduced to Captain Wynter and the other people concerned with the production. I soon found myself prancing about with the chorus men, learning the job!

I ought to mention here that I had come straight from the amateur dramatic circles of Manchester to Singapore. I had been something of a hit there in the previous two years, and had played many principal parts. I had, in fact, like so many other businessmen in Manchester at that time, been semi-professional—that is to say, had received money for my services, both on the stage and the concert platform.

I mention this fact merely to show how I managed to get an extra bit of fun out of this first show in Singapore by pretending I was a new hand at the game.

It was at these rehearsals that I met Whitefield, whom I later lived with at Zetland House.

The orchestra was conducted by A.P. Ager, (who has only lately retired from *The Straits Times*,) a violin player of no mean ability. He still plays, I understand, in some of the well-known orchestras in London. Wallace, who played in the first violins, is still here; Major St Clair played the string bass and Whitefield was at the piano and accompanied during rehearsals.

The play was duly produced and according to reports was a great success. I have before me as I write the cutting from the paper criticising the first performance, and it is most amusing to read, after so very many years of stage producing, that the troubles that existed then have been very much the same all along and, allowing for the higher standard required and expected, are very much the same today.

Here are the opening sentences of the paper's report:

'The production of musical plays in Singapore, in common with most places east of Suez, is fraught with many difficulties. In the first place the supply of voices is strictly limited, more especially when a modicum of dramatic talent, in addition to a voice of even the most moderate dimensions, is sought after in one female form divine. Add to this the necessity for an averagely good "stage appearance", take into account the petty little social jealousies that prohibit the simultaneous appearance of Mrs X and Mrs Y on the same stage, bear in mind that unless the performance takes place within certain limits of time the Misses Z will have accompanied their uncle to Europe, and then start in and produce a musical play.'

In the last act the chorus men had to make up as prominent citizens of Singapore. They got me up to represent Sir Alexander Swettenham. I had never seen him, nor did I ever see him afterwards to my knowledge, but I was told it was a good burlesque. H.W. Noon as Daddy Abrams, in a suit borrowed for the occasion from Daddy, and A.B. Cross as C.B. Buckley were the two that 'brought down the house'.

Life was much more intimate in those days, and this kind of thing was taken in good part. I wonder what would happen today if I were to bring onto the stage a burlesque chorus made up to represent the 'highs' of present Singapore!

As I have said previously, I joined the cathedral choir the week after the funeral of Queen Victoria and one day after I joined the chorus of the opera. Tonkin was also responsible for this, and he took me along. He had evidently heard me singing as I stood next to him on the stage. It was at that first choir practice that I met the great Mr Buckley, C.B. as we called him, a man who was unique. I was privileged to know him well from that time onwards and to be allowed to help him in many of his efforts for the good of the children and poor people of this place. I maintain, and always shall do so, that Buckley was one of the greatest men that Singapore has had as a resident. The portrait of him in the Memorial Hall, painted by one of the sons of Sir William Adamson of Adamson Gilfillan (as the firm is now called) is an excellent one, and to my mind seems to portray, in its quiet colour, the nature of a man who strove hard all his life to do little things well. I suppose no man was better loved by the local-born, and many who have grown to middle age by now will remember him and his good works with gratitude and respect.

My first introduction to him was typical. He was choirmaster when I joined the choir, and a certain anthem that was being practised had a small solo in it. 'Who'll sing this?' said Buckley. Tonkin, feeling I suppose that he must look after his protégé, said, 'Why not give it to Brown?'

'Brown, Brown,' said C.B. chewing his handkerchief as usual. 'Never heard of him, *he can't sing*. Who is he?' However, I sang the solo and so brought myself to the notice of Mr Edward

Salzmann who was sitting behind me at the organ. And then began a friendship with him and his wife and family that never faltered, never was broken, until death itself cut the chain. How good they were to me in those days! Almost every Sunday after church they would have me up to dinner; Edward would play my songs for me and I would meet new people there and make new friends. At times, too, when the old man—for even then he was in his sixties—was in a reminiscent mood, I would sit on the veranda with him while he yarned away of London in the Sixties; of Sir Michael Costa; the Royal Italian Opera Company; of all the great singers that were but a name to me; of that curious Bohemian life of musical London in the days before England discovered—or rather rediscovered—that she had a musical soul of her own.

Wonderful talks and wonderful evenings, and I think that Salzmann and I got to understand each other then in a way that was to keep our friendship strong when the time came for me to be called upon to bring my more modern ideas to bear upon the musical life in Singapore and, as it were, to supersede him. For Salzmann was conservative. He hated new things. The music he had lived in and on in London was to his mind the best, and he would not believe that the best of his day could perhaps be bettered by the best of later days. I remember that he would never say a good word about the fine organ that we built in the cathedral to replace the Walker organ that he had played on for so long. He didn't understand it. Pneumatic action was foreign to him. He had played tracker action organs all his life, and the entirely different 'touch' used to annoy him every time he played for a wedding (which was all he did after his retirement).

Modern harmonies, too, used to irritate him, and I remember having a big argument with him at his house one Sunday night when I was practising a song for a concert he was putting together. He refused to play a certain chord as it was written because he said it was wrong. I, knowing him well enough by that time, insisted that he should do so. In the end, as neither would give way, we chose another song!

About my experiences in the cathedral choir I shall have more to say at various places in this narrative. A history of the music in St Andrew's Cathedral, written by me at the time of the dedication of the new organ in 1931, is available, and will be of interest to many who have worshipped in the churches of England that have existed here since the colony was founded.

It seems appropriate here to give some description of the town and suburbs of Singapore as they were in the first year of the present century. It must be remembered that the business of the port was of a very different description from what it is today. At that time Singapore was the trading centre for all the eastern islands. From Borneo, from Java, from Manila, from the Celebes, from as far away as Timor and New Guinea, native boats brought the produce of the East to the godowns of Singapore, and took away with them the manufactured goods of the West. Some, in fact the majority, of the native trade was pure barter, and the quantity and variety of the produce dealt in made the life of the man on the produce side of a firm a very interesting and varied one. On the import side one had to know the tastes of the natives of practically all the islands of the East, and very often had to anticipate and even manufacture those tastes.

Saigon trade, owing to the French duties in Indo–China, had gone from us a year or so before this, but the Bangkok trade—later to be the most important of all the markets—was just beginning. The range of articles dealt in by an average import firm varied from eight and a quarter pounds of grey shirting to nice lines in fancy spittoons, and from forties grey yarn in ten pound bundles (really ten pounds in those days) to umbrellas, felt hats and bedsteads. Truly an alarming list! And all these articles had their own particular market; many of them would only be required at one particular season of the year, and it required a nice discrimination to have the right stuff, and just the right amount of it, in stock at the right time.

I suppose there are very few people working in the big firms out here today who remember the arrival of the Bugis fleet. Apart altogether from its business importance, the arrival of that fleet was a very wonderful sight.

Picture to yourself a forest of sail appearing over the horizon away towards Riau. Imagine the sea in that direction gradually becoming covered with small native schooners—Bugis boats as they were called—until as far as the eye could see there seemed to be nothing but masts and sails. A wonderful sight it was to watch that fleet sail in—I have seen as many as 300 boats—and how we used to watch for them! A tamby was always stationed on the veranda by the telescope to give the signal as soon as they appeared, and when they came to an anchor off Tanjong Rhu and

Clyde Terrace, the harbour presented a most animated appearance. And when it is remembered that those boats contained the fruits of a year's labour of the people of the Celebes and round about, and that they had come to barter that produce for the sarongs and prints, the pots and pans, the nails and hammers and all the hundred and one things that made life worth living where they came from, it can be imagined how the town hummed with activity. And, remember also, that what went on with the Bugis was going on every day with some other parts of the eastern seas. Native craft of all kinds and from all places concentrated on Singapore. Here were the big steamers, ready to carry away the gathered produce to all parts of the Western world. Here were the great stores, full of things that a native wanted but could not make himself. Nowhere else in these eastern waters, at that time, was there such a centre of trade and activity. Truly, the name The Gateway of the East was fully deserved.

And we worked much harder, too. I am not saying this because it sounds nice, but just as a simple fact. From nine o'clock every day till five or five-thirty at the earliest (unless we *asked* to be allowed to leave a bit earlier), till three to four o'clock on Saturdays, and twenty minutes or so for tiffin—taken in the office—with the frequent risk of being called out to attend to a dealer, was the usual régime. Mark you, everyone from Tuan Besar to the newest-joined assistant brought his tiffin down to the office in a tiffin basket. The senior men would have their days to go over to the Singapore Club to tiffin and to meet others of their standing but, generally speaking, Singapore in those days could be said to tiffin at its work!

And good fun we used to have, too. Very good curry used to be obtained from the hawkers in the five-foot way, and we used to toss to see who should provide the staff with a plate each. In the mangosteen season, too, there was great fun to be had. Collyer Quay was then only less than half the width of what it is today, and there was no reclaimed land beyond. The *tongkang* used to come up alongside the sea wall and load the goods for the steamers direct from the godowns.

After tiffin, if we had a few minutes to spare, we used to collect all the mangosteen skins and go onto the veranda, and take pot shots at the coolies working in the boats and along the sea wall. A well-directed shot would often cause consternation among the boatmen and sometimes, if the source of the missile was unknown, a free fight, to our great delight. We would vary this by pelting the staff of a neighbouring godown who were on their veranda doing the same thing! Sometimes eggs that looked rather too hoary to eat would find themselves among the ammunition. They were always reserved for the *tongkang* men!

As I have said, Collyer Quay was a very different place then from what it is today. Those verandas I have spoken of were continuous affairs, and ran past every office. A portion of the original is still seen over the premises of the P&O Bank in Prince Street. Getting onto the veranda at the corner of Prince Street and de Souza Street, one could walk right round almost to where Change Alley and Collyer meet. Gilfillan, Wood & Co. (now Adamson Gilfillan) had, if I remember rightly, a veranda of their own which did not join onto the rest.

Then the 'outside way' started again the other side of Change Alley, and went on to the Hong Kong Bank.

Among the firms that were supplied with this extra footpath were Drew & Napier, Paterson Simons, Guthrie & Co., Brinkmann & Co., Huttenbach Bros., Syme & Co. and Kumpers & Co. On the other side of Change Alley there were, among others, Rautenberg, Schmidt & Co., Hooglandt & Co., Diethelm & Co. and Boustead & Co. The Borneo Company was then, and until comparatively recently, in Finlayson Green and was about the only big firm that did not possess offices on Collyer Quay. Behn Meyer & Co. were, of course, where Holt's building stands today.

The reason for this concentration on the front is obvious. In the old days, before the era of steam or electricity, the sailing vessels anchored in the roads and loaded and unloaded there. Firms had to be in a position from where they could scan the horizon for the arrival of ships and when I came to Singapore every firm still had its telescope on the veranda, a relic of the days of sail. When steam and wireless came in, this necessity for a 'front seat' disappeared, and now there are very few of the old firms left in their original habitat.

Guthrie & Co. were, I think, the first to go and others followed them in quick succession. The Arcade was built, cutting the veranda footpath in half, then Winchester House (these two buildings being, I think, the first three-storied buildings in the town), then St Helen's Court, on the spot where Brinkmann used to be and lastly the entire pier end of the frontage was altered by the erection of Union Building and the new Hong Kong Bank.

Farther along the front there was, in 1901, the open space in front of Johnston's Pier, and there the road ended. The sea came right up to the walls of the Chamber of Commerce building, above which was the old Singapore Club—with the inevitable veranda. The post office was behind this building, and the only way onto Collyer Quay at that end was via the Cavenagh Suspension Bridge. At the point of the river on what had been, till a few years before I came, Fort Fullerton, stood the drill hall, the identical building that was afterwards removed to Beach Road and has only just lately disappeared to give place to the new imposing headquarters of the SVC. The gun mountings of the old muzzle-loaders were still in position when I joined the Volunteers.

Raffles Square was very much the same size as it is today, but had a vastly different appearance. Sometimes, looking out of a fourth- or fifth-storey window onto the glaring whiteness of the square with its motorcars parked in orderly ranks in the centre, my mind goes back to the old days—the red laterite roads, the big shady flame-of-the-forest trees in the centre, the horses and victorias standing under them for shelter from the sun while the 'mems' did their shopping; and I wonder if we are any better off now—with all the present-day amenities—than we were then? Life was slower, more leisurely, there was not the rush and strain of the present age. Amusement was a thing to be looked forward to, talked about and prepared for—not an everyday occurrence demanded as a right. Certainly we had no fans, only *punkahs*; oil lamps were our lighting mainstay. No electricity whatsoever (except the telephone) was available and we all had to wear blue suits to go to church in! The ladies wore high-necked blouses, flowing skirts with lots of petticoats and long, kid or suede gloves. But in the offices men—from the Tuan Besar downwards—wore the white suit, the *baju tutup*; collars were never seen except at parties, the races or in church.

I remember well the first time a man came to afternoon service in the cathedral in a white suit! It was the parson himself! The Rev. H.G. Peile, now dean of the cathedral at St John's, Newfoundland, was a man standing about six feet four inches. He was a splendid type of up-to-date Christian, with a modern young man's contempt for the smug respectability of the Victorian era— which still had a hold on this place when he came. He turned up in church one day to the horror of the congregation with a pair of white trousers showing beneath his cassock! But he broke the tradition!

That was, however, some years later when traditions were ripe for breaking. At the time I am speaking of, viz 1901, they were still exercising complete sway over Singapore society.

One of the pet fetishes of the place was the question of smoking. A pipe, such a common sight since the Great War, was only conspicuous by its absence. In fact it was looked upon with disgust and no well-mannered gentleman would think of smoking one in the presence of other people! Pipes *were* smoked, of course, but only by people like seafaring men and those weird people from Lancashire known as 'piece-goods men', in which category I came! Even in the Cricket Club itself a pipe was not considered

43

'the right thing', while to dare to smoke one in the office was to risk a very severe reprimand.

I remember one Saturday afternoon going to the Ladies' Lawn Tennis Club to play with Arthur Barker, Noon and Tonkin. The club was then the centre of society life. Men were only admitted 'on sufferance' and had no standing as members, and it was considered to be a certificate of merit to be allowed to become a subscriber.

On Saturday afternoons the club was generally deserted, it being the day for tennis at home. On this particular occasion Noon and myself, going to the lawn in rickshaws, had lit our pipes and, the club being deserted when we got there, had not bothered to put them out but had walked out to our court with them in our mouths. As we sauntered over we noticed a lady get out of her carriage and enter the club, evidently calling for something she had left for she went away again immediately. But she was there long enough to see us, and next day we received an intimation that if we were seen smoking pipes again on the premises we would have to resign! And there wasn't a soul in the club or on the courts and we were in the open air! Think of it, you pipe smokers, and compare those days with these!

I remember, too, the day when Borneo Bill, otherwise known as Robertson, a partner in Lyall & Evatt, dared to smoke a pipe at the races! Funny days, weren't they?

But I am wandering. I was giving some description of the place as it was in 1901.

Going over Cavenagh Bridge one would notice at low tide a

great rock sticking up in the centre of the river, on the sea side of the bridge. Various attempts had been made to get rid of this, and even in 1901 the papers were reporting another attempt by blasting. It was finally removed when the Anderson Bridge was thrown across.

The government buildings were the same outside as they are today—except for the portion where the Treasury Office now is which was added later—and I expect they were just as dirty and disreputable inside.

The old town hall was where the theatre is today, and the Cricket Club then in existence was on the same site as the present one. On the esplanade, the sea side, was that mysterious obelisk now on the plot of land near the river and between the two bridges. Its real name is the Dalhousie Monument, and it has been moved about so often that it is a wonder that it didn't disappear long ago. It was originally erected to mark the spot where the only governor of the old John Company to visit Singapore landed in the mud. This seems to have been somewhere near where Anderson Bridge is today, but the monument was moved from there later to a position approximate to the present Marine Police headquarters. When I came I think it was where the cenotaph now stands, and later on it stood in the centre of Empress Place. Now it is back nearer to the spot it commemorates than it has been for very many years.

Raffles' statue, now in front of the Victoria Memorial buildings, stood in the centre of the esplanade, and incidentally made an excellent grandstand for Malay boys at a football match.

The old Europe Hotel was a funny building. At the corner of High Street and running along the front of what is now called St Andrew's Road was a low, one-storied, large-verandaed room. On the whitewashed wall of this in large black letters was painted the inscription: BAR AND BILLIARD ROOM. It was a great place for tourists of the non-British races, and when a French mail service was in it was, at times, a somewhat startling sight. On the veranda at night there were frequent quarrels, and it was the pleasant custom of the one who had the better of the quarrel to throw his vanquished opponent over the railing onto the footpath below! The entrance to the hotel proper was through a gateway at the end of this building. The dining room was in the big building immediately in front of this gateway and then, set back from the road, a two-storied building ran right along to Coleman Street. Half of this contained the bedrooms of the hotel, and the other half the municipal offices.

The Recreation Club (a very small building then) and Raffles Hotel stood where they do today.

The Sailors' Home was at the corner of North Bridge Road and Stamford Road, and halfway between this building and Coleman Street was a hole in the wall where the only fire engine the town possessed used to be kept. The horses were stabled in Abrams' yard, first in Bras Basah Road and then in Orchard Road. The chief of the fire brigade was G.P. Owen who lived at Thompson Road Reservoir, and by the time he had got into his uniform and driven down from there to let the engine out, the fire was either out or had done its work!

The Adelphi Hotel was in existence, on the same site as the present day, but it was considered a very second-rate place and was the resort mainly of foreigners.

In North Bridge Road, just past Bras Basah Road and on the left-hand side going out, was the celebrated Tingel Tangel. This was, in fact, a local edition of a continental dance hall. It was kept by an old Austrian named Hackmeier, and sported a ladies' orchestra! The girls in the orchestra were Austrians and Poles and were carefully looked after. In spite of rumours that went around they were, I believe, at all events at the time of which I am writing, quite respectable. Several of them married quite well.

The Tingel Tangel was the resort of all the young bloods—and some of the older ones, too—who were making a night of it. One went there, drank beer and paid fifty cents a time to dance with one of the band girls! The place was also a favourite rendezvous for the officers and men of the foreign ships, naval and otherwise, that frequented the port.

And though the members of the orchestra were respectable, I am very much afraid that the same could not always be said for Hackmeier's clientele. A sure and certain way of starting trouble was to walk inside, shut the door and shout, 'Squarehead!' The war of the nations—in miniature—then started immediately! How many times a year old Hackmeier replaced his furniture, history does not record!

The best (?) episode that I remember in connection with the Tingel Tangel concerns a gentleman—now retired—who was very well known indeed in Singapore. I wonder if he will recall the incident if he reads this.

One day, having been presented with some half-dozen geese by native merchants—it was probably Chinese New Year—he decided to have some fun. So with a pal or two he set out in a gharry for the Tingel Tangel with the geese in their baskets on top.

Arriving at the entrance they seized the baskets, rushed into the dancing room, let loose the geese and, with the usual battle cry of 'Squarehead!', waded in. I was not there but I was told that the pandemonium occasioned by the fighting and the flying squawking geese gave great satisfaction to those seeking entertainment, and altogether it was voted a very excellent evening's amusement!

The Tingel Tangel fell on evil days later on. Changes in ideas as to what was a 'nice' evening resulted in the place being left to the tender mercies of the very much lower orders. It was still going, however, when the war broke out and old Hackmeier, his wife and those members of the band who hadn't got away in time were interned in Kuala Lumpur. I brought them down from there during the 1915 Singapore Mutiny, but I do not think I could have given them then the certificate of respectability that they certainly would have earned some ten or fifteen years previously.

In 1901 Raffles Hotel stood where it does now. It consisted of the central block and, I think, some or all of the rooms round the lawn. The Bras Basah Road portion was not in existence, and where the annexe is now was a billiard room.

Orchard Road was then, as today, the principal traffic outlet from the town. Native shops were on either side, starting from

Dhoby Ghaut and going as far as Cavenagh Road. The notable exceptions to shops were, on the left going out, Abrams' Horse Repository at the corner of Tank Road—the dilapidated buildings of which still stand—and Dallans' Horse Repository where the market and Cold Storage are now. These two were the principal suppliers of one of the most necessary adjuncts to life out here—transport; and they must have done a very flourishing trade for many years. I shall have more to say of the genial Daddy Abrams and his delightful family later on.

After Dallans' place, Orchard Road became residential. The railway, of course, was not built till later and at Emerald Hill there were big European houses with large compounds. If I remember rightly Pierce, the municipal engineer, lived there and the containing hedge of his compound came down to the road just about where the railway bridge was later.

The residential districts were much the same, as regards the principal roads, as they are today. Many of the houses remain, some have been rebuilt and, in some cases, big compounds cut up into smaller ones, but Grange Road, for instance, Scotts Road, Stevens Road, Balmoral Road and River Valley Road show extraordinarily little change in the thirty years or so that I have known them. Red laterite roads have given place to macadam and tarmac, and houses have sprung up and been renovated or pulled down, but the old trees and hedges are still there and the 'atmosphere' of the roads remains unaltered.

The expansion of the suburbs has, of course, been great. New roads have been cut—notably Nassim Road, Anderson Road,

Grove Road and many others—while entirely new suburbs have sprung up in places like Grove Estate, Katong, Holland Road and Pasir Panjang.

The native parts of the city remained much the same for many years. In fact even today, if one stood on Cavenagh Bridge with a picture postcard of thirty years ago in one's hand and compared it with the view upriver, very little difference would be noticed.

The advent of the 'back lane' scheme, however, and later the clearance of the slum areas are making definite changes nowadays. There are large tracts of the town, and will be more as time goes on, which present a very different appearance from the dirty, unhealthy and ill-ventilated places that served the native population for shops and houses in 1901.

3

1901 (Continued)

I have, in a previous chapter, mentioned the fire brigade, or rather the apology for one. In March 1901 Mr Arthur Barker was made a local director of the Commercial Union Insurance Company, and in that capacity, and in his other capacity of a commissioner, he began to press the municipality for a drastic revision of the fire-fighting methods of the town.

There had been a big fire in Malacca Street, where evidently the existing methods did not meet with the approval of the insurance people. Among other things it was alleged that many tons of water had been pumped into a building nearby the one that had been on fire, but about twelve hours after the real fire had been extinguished! This was, I think, the beginning of the agitation that eventually was to see the removal of Mr Pett and the organisation of a professional brigade that was to grow into one of the smartest and most efficient brigades in the East. The agitation, however, went on for some time before Pett was removed. He left Singapore after some years of work here, and went up to Shanghai to assume the position of head of the brigade there.

In looking through the old papers of about this time, I see a notice that about April time Mr W.H. Read, CMG, brought out a book entitled *Play and Politics*, reminiscences of Malaya. Mr Read, so often mentioned in Buckley's book, was one of the greatest of the old Singaporeans. He was a member of the first Legislative Council that existed here, and attended the first meeting on 1 April 1867. He was a leading spirit in the colony in everything, from government to amateur dramatics. He must have been a very old man when he published his reminiscences.

On Saturday, 6 April I made my first appearance on a concert platform in Singapore. I had sung privately at the Tanglin Club for the Salzmanns before this, but it was at a farewell concert organised to say goodbye to W. Makepeace who was going on leave, that my first public appearance was made.

At that concert I sang a song that had been given to me in Manchester by a young fellow called Ernest Hastings, who had been in the habit of playing for me at times. Today, Ernest Hastings is very well known to the home public for his songs at the piano and he has, I believe, made a great name for himself. The song was called 'The Commissionaire' and was written originally for a Manchester pantomime.

Of the numerous fellows whose names appear on that programme with me, I am the only one now left in Singapore.

I met about this time the great John Roberts, of billiard fame. He passed through Singapore and gave some exhibition games and, like most of these people, came up to dine one night at Zetland House. He was an old man then but I saw him play, and can remember the fascination of this 'wizardry'. He played against Dr Mugliston, the father of Gerald, and a Mr C.E. Velge, who I think was the registrar at the Supreme Court at the time.

There seems to have been a fairly vigorous outcry in the year 1901 against the 'innovations', as they were called, at St Andrew's Cathedral. Allegations were made that confession was being practised, and a certain person wrote to the papers that, though a notice hung in the church said that: THIS CHURCH IS OPEN DAILY FROM SEVEN O'CLOCK IN THE MORNING TO FIVE O'CLOCK IN THE EVENING, he went there one day at three in the afternoon and found every door shut except the vestry door, at which was stationed a Chinese caretaker who told him he couldn't see the chaplain as he was at prayer with another person!

Another said that he had seceded from the Roman Church and joined the Church of England because he couldn't stand the 'mummeries and ceremonies' of the former, but that now he thought of going back again because the cathedral was getting worse than the Romans in this respect.

Another suggested some method of dealing with the priests who practised these 'heresies', but the paper, in a footnote, said that it could not print the suggestions because they were 'so decisively drastic as to be unpresentable'!

It makes one smile to read these old letters, and to realise that all through the years the same trouble has gone on. It is mainly owing to the good sense of the majority of the chaplains in charge that the services at the cathedral have remained broad and acceptable to all people. The ritualistic movement has endeavoured, at times, to thrust itself on the cathedral, sometimes with ecclesiastical backing behind it, but up to the present it has not had much success. One hopes that, for the sake of the various classes of church opinion that worship in our only church, it never will have any.

It is interesting to note, however, that Archdeacon Perham, who was still here when I arrived, had lately introduced the choral communion to the cathedral. He was so universally loved that he was able to do it successfully, but for a long time he had bitter opponents, and one of them was his own organist, Mr Salzmann.

It might be advisable that a book should be kept by the chaplains in which these records of disagreement could be filed. It might help new clergy to get a better grasp of the style of parish they have to deal with than some of them, in my time, seem to have obtained!

In Singapore there was, at this time, a curious fellow who styled himself Baron de Horn. By 1901 he had fallen upon evil days, but there had been a time when he seemed to have plenty of cash (or at all events, credit), had entertained the governors and officials to sumptuous repasts, had driven 'four in hand' to the races and generally made his presence felt. He insisted that he was a son of the Czar of Russia, and in an office in Change Alley he kept a mysterious ironbound chest, which he said contained a portion of the Russian crown jewels. In April 1901, however, he was living at Katong and was brought up before the magistrate and bound over for firing at an Indian whom he said had been trespassing in his compound. I forget what happened to him in the end, but he certainly provided plenty of food for gossip in his day.

There was another character knocking about the town, too, at this time: a mad Irishman who had adopted the Chittiar religion, and who used to go about Collyer Quay in the somewhat gauzy and inadequate garb affected by those of his adopted sect. It was curious to see his shaven head and perfectly white skin. I knew him quite well, and often used to talk to him.

On Sunday, 21 April the Duke and Duchess of Cornwall and York arrived on the SS *Ophir* on their way to Australia.

This visit had been looked forward to for many months, and most elaborate preparations had been made to give a splendid welcome to the royal visitors.

It is not my intention to describe the visit in its entirety, but merely to give personal reminiscences of that interesting event.

I was helping Mr Salzmann in his arrangements for getting together and rehearsing the choir of welcome—for I had not at that time joined the Volunteers. The choir—about a hundred strong—was seated on a specially erected platform at the end of the town hall and the Duke and Duchess, with the governor, were to sit on a dais in front of the orchestra. I remember that sarcastic letters were written to the papers by clever people who pointed out that this position was obviously wrong, for if the royal visitors faced the audience they would have their backs to the choir, who were to do the welcoming. If they sat facing the choir the big audience who were to witness the presentation of addresses would be at their rear.

One wag suggested that they might sit facing the audience

and turn their heads round when the choir sang, risking a crick in the neck by so doing! Of course, it is quite obvious that the proper place for the choir ought to have been *at the back of* the audience, but no one seemed to think of that, and when the time came we duly sang our songs of welcome to the royal backs.

According to the papers, a glorious muddle occurred regarding the arrival of the SS *Ophir*. She steamed alongside the Borneo Wharf at about half past six on that Sunday morning, and apart from Mr Seller, the manager of the Tanjong Pagar Dock Company, Mr Niven, the secretary, a few minor officials and some coolies, no one saw her arrive.

When the gangway was let down, the first man to go on board was Major St Clair. Seven-thirty in the morning came and there was still no sign of any government officials, but Mr Grigor Taylor, the head of the Telegraph Company, and Mr Tom Scott of Guthrie & Co. had turned up and gone on board, though what they did when they got there I don't know!

Soon afterwards the master attendant and the chief boarding officer arrived, and by this time the royal party seemed to be waking up. Prince Alexander of Teck was seen walking about the deck, and Mrs Derek Keppel amused herself by taking snapshots of the wharf. The Duke himself came out of his room, sat himself down in a deckchair and commenced to read the paper! At eight o'clock a bit of excitement was caused by the hoisting of the Union Jack aft, to the strains of the national anthem played by the band of the Royal Marines, which was on board, and then things settled down again!

At length the private secretary to the governor came and the programme commenced, only to be interrupted again at ten o'clock when the *Ophir* signalled to the *St George*, the escorting cruiser, for the royal barge only to be told that it wasn't available as they had forgotten to get steam up!

After waiting about half an hour, the royal party began to get fed up so a passing Tanjong Pagar dock tug, the *Albuquerque*, was hailed to go alongside, and it was intimated that the royal party would use her to go to Johnston's Pier. The harbour flag was hauled down, the royal standard hoisted in its place and the Duke and Duchess were just stepping onto the gangway to go aboard when the *St George* signalled that steam was up on the royal barge. The Tanjong Pagar tug didn't have the unexpected honour after all!

I was on the veranda of the old town hall, from where an excellent view over Cavenagh Bridge to the pier could be obtained. All troops were in position at the scheduled time, and it was a blazing hot day. In those days the navy wore straw hats, not topees, and unfortunately they were lining the bridge and its approaches where no shade was to be obtained. The long delay occasioned by the events just recorded proved too much for the troops, and the sun claimed very many victims in the ranks of both the navy and army, though, if I remember rightly, the Volunteers came through all right.

Finally the procession came. The royal carriage was headed by a mounted detachment of Sikhs in scarlet uniforms known as the Perak Lancers, a private bodyguard of about twenty men and an officer, maintained by the Sultan of Perak and lent to Singapore for this occasion.

The ceremony in the town hall, in which Salzmann's choir took part, was held on the Monday morning. It is interesting to note that it was said by many afterwards that, of all the distinguished people gathered that day in the hall, the most distinguished-looking was Mr Salzmann himself! At the close of the ceremony we sang a chorus from Handel's *Solomon*, entitled 'From the East unto the West', which I had never heard before nor have I come across it since.

I was not present at the children's reception, though Mr Buckley had asked me to help. I was to step into his shoes in this respect some twenty years later, when the present royal visitors' son came to Singapore. That same afternoon the lovely full orchestra of the Royal Marines (Chatham Division), under the direction of Mr J. Wright, gave a concert at the Teutonia Club, probably one of the greatest musical treats that Singapore has ever experienced.

That evening there was a reception at Government House to which practically everyone was invited. It was of the usual kind and was followed by the inevitable Chinese welcome—a torchlight procession. One incident of the reception stands out in my mind. It was only when we got up to Government House that the news went round that those shaking hands with the royal party would have to wear white gloves. The ladies, of course, were all right—they always wore gloves in the evening in those days—but what about the poor men? If there had been a dance afterwards we would have come prepared but as it was, only about a dozen pairs of gloves were found to be available. The difficulty was cleverly got around by stationing a chain of men *behind* the royal chairs. The gloves were then dealt out in 'ones' to the first twenty-four to be received, and as each man passed the Duchess, the man at the end of the chain pulled the glove off the wearer's hand, passed it down the line and handed it to one of the waiting guests. Men who got a left-hand glove had to wear it back to front! Great days, those!

I saw the procession of rickshaws round Chinatown on the Sunday evening from a shop in Kling Street (now Chulia Street). The owner of the shop was a very big dealer, and all the import men in the place seemed to be congregated there. We were regaled with a large quantity of liquid refreshments while waiting. Kling Street was completely paved with Turkey-red cloth, while there was a complete ceiling of the same cloth stretching from rooftop to rooftop across the whole length of the street. The Chinese dealers knew how to do things properly in those days. The rickshaw pullers were clothed in scarlet running pants and scarlet coats for the occasion. I remember that the Duke looked quite at home in his rickshaw, but the Duchess sat up very stiffly and seemed *most* uncomfortable, as if she expected to be thrown out at any moment!

The royal party left on Tuesday, and I had the honour of being invited to tiffin that day on the *St George*—why, I don't know, because I was only a youngster at the time. From the quarterdeck of the cruiser I watched the finest Malay *koleh* races

I have ever seen—big boats containing thirty or forty men apiece. One of them, in rounding the stern of the *St George*, completely capsized.

And so ended my first experience of a royal visit to Singapore.

The present Victoria Memorial Hall, which remained a white elephant for so many years, first came before the public eye at a meeting held in May of 1901. Various suggestions were put forward as to what form the memorial to the late Queen should take. The first proposal, to build a theatre, was vetoed by the Chinese delegates at a meeting called to consider the matter; a statue, proposed by the municipality, was vetoed by the governor who said, firstly, that unless it was designed by a world-famous artist no one would look at it, and secondly, that there would be something repugnant to the native mind in exposing to the rain, wind and sun a statue of a woman who had been so loved and revered by all. Two very sound reasons, I think, and typical of the excellent common sense which was one of Sir Frank Swettenham's greatest attributes. Finally a memorial hall was agreed upon. Some years later the PWD commenced operations upon the building and got the walls about six feet above the ground, where they remained for some time. Then the work was handed over to Swan & McLaren to finish. It may have been totally untrue, but it was said at the time that the PWD had to give the work up because it was too big for them—they could not visualise so large a building!

Registration of domestic servants was a great topic for the

controversialists at this time, and the argument, with variations, has gone on up to the present day. Personally it has always been my experience that people got the kind of servants they deserved, and I have never had any fault to find with the Chinese house servants; they have always seemed to me to be extraordinarily willing and faithful, and ready to do anything to help. I may have been lucky, but I have had only three boys in about twenty years, one *amah* in twenty-three years and a cook since soon after I was married, who would come back to me today if I required his services, so perhaps I am prejudiced.

Soon after the Duke and Duchess left Singapore I joined the Volunteers. As a matter of fact, I joined the Singapore Volunteer Rifles having a preference for the infantry, but at the time I joined, the artillery was very short of men, and Major St Clair, whom I now knew well, and a Lieutenant Hilton of the Borneo Company—a Manchester man—tried hard to get me to join the SVA. Indeed, I believe one or other of them must have been so sure of me that they went and entered my name as a recruit in the SVA books at the drill hall. The consequence was that, when the time came for me to be presented with the Officers' Volunteer decoration some twenty-three years later, and my record had to be made out, I found that I had started in the SVA, a corps to which I never belonged. I had not joined the SVR until a much later date, my own company commander having evidently forgotten to put my name down in the records! Finally, I'm afraid, the authorities had to take my word for it!

Volunteering in those days was a very different thing from

what it is today. We were keen enough—we must have been to put up with what we had to undergo—but there was no systematic training, no insistence of efficiency on the part of the commissioned officers, and we were really terribly mishandled by our commanders on the whole, though there were one or two notable exceptions.

It would be impossible to recount all the things that went on and what we did, but I have gathered together a few of the more laughable incidents of these days under articles headed, 'The Bad Old Days', which have appeared as 'turnovers' in the *Singapore Free Press*.

I had, by this time, joined the Philharmonic Society, and I attended the annual meeting that was held in May. The society was on a downward spiral when I joined it, and soon after this the choral section disappeared, never to be resuscitated properly though many attempts were made.

St Clair, though a good fellow in many respects and full of musical enthusiasm, was not at his best in handling the ladies, and I think the incident that finally disbanded the chorus was the following:

In those days the town hall was lit by gas, a vertical pipe hanging from the roof having a horizontal T piece at the bottom, from each end of which three gas jets sprang.

The ladies had not been singing their best that evening, and St Clair got more and more annoyed with them. Finally, losing his temper, he put down his baton and addressed them somewhat in this fashion:

'Ladies, you can't sing and you're not a bit of good in the choir. You might get up on these'—pointing to the gas brackets—'and give a horizontal-bar display. You would be quite as good at it as you are at singing, and the men would be much more amused!'

Needless to say, the ladies walked out in a body and didn't came back for some time!

The chances of entertainment outside what we made ourselves were few and far between. One thing we had then, though, which we seldom get now, was a good circus. Two used to frequent these parts: Harmstons (still remembered) and Warrens (now, I am afraid, forgotten). Of the two, the former was by far the best and everyone, from the governor downwards, could be found sitting round the sawdust ring.

Old Mrs Harmston was a motherly old lady and had two children: Nellie, a very pretty girl, and a son. They used to do a dual act on horses and were very clever. I think Nellie married happily in these parts; she deserved to for she was very nice. Circus people are noted, of course, for their simple lives and homely ways, and the Harmstons were no exception to the rule. The old mother had managed to give her children a very good education.

Sometimes these two shows, in the course of their itinerary, used to arrive in Singapore together, and their attempts to outrival each other in extravagant advertisements of their respective merits were most amusing. I have before me the advertisements of the two of them at a period when their visits clashed. Warrens called itself:

'A stupendous federation of the world's wonders; a sterling diverting electric success, successful beyond the most extravagant praise.'

I think, however, that Harmstons won on points this time, because it called itself:

'A monument of progress, prosperity and business integrity, unequalled, unapproachable, the MASTODON of modern amusement enterprise.'

The word 'mastodon' is distinctly good, I think.

The lads of the village always used to have some fun when the visits of the circus came round.

On one occasion about eight of them hired a gharry and bought tin trumpets and a toy drum or two. Getting rid of the gharry driver, they loaded up with four inside, two on the top, one driving and one sitting on the ledge at the back. They then drove straight through the box office, into the big tent and to the right, where they drove round and round to the accompaniment of cheers from the audience. Mrs Harmston and her husband, old 'Colonel' Bob Love, used to take these interruptions in very good humour. In fact I think they rather liked it as it enhanced their popularity.

I played the first tournament game of lawn bowls that I had ever played in my life on Friday, 31 May. I was drawn against H.G. Diss, then in charge of the tailoring department of John Little. He was a celebrated figure in the town and afterwards head of his own firm in Conduit Street. W. Diss was also a clever actor and sang a good comic song, and when I saw him years later in his

London establishment he seemed to have changed very little from the Diss of Singapore days.

4

1901 (Concluded)

Nowadays one very seldom hears of an amok, that dreaded disease which seems to affect only the native races of the East and causes in its victim a passion for murder and a lust for blood.

There was a very terrible case in June of this year. I just escaped being mixed up in it as I arrived at the Beach Road police station, on my way to Arab Street, just as a man in a dying condition was being taken in there.

He broke out in a house in Little Cross Street and, arming himself with a sharp spearhead attached to a long pole, attacked and killed a woman. Then, breaking down a partition, he went for the other occupants of the house, a Malay family. Only two of these escaped. From the house the murderer made his way into the street and so savagely attacked a little boy who was walking quietly along that he died from his injuries. From this point the murderer's course took him along Arab Street and into Haji Lane, a trail of wounded and dead left in his wake. How he was stopped is not known, but a Bengali policeman found him lying wounded in a drain, disarmed him and sat on him till help arrived. He died as he was entering the police station.

This was, I think, the worst case that ever came to my immediate attention. As I have said, the disease is seldom heard of nowadays.

On 6 July there appeared in the papers a large advertisement announcing the forthcoming visit of that new wonder of the world, the biograph! It was the first time that moving pictures had been shown in these parts, and the owners were touring the East showing views of the Queen's funeral, scenes from the Second Boer War, etc. Prices of admission were S$3, S$2 and S$1, and I've no doubt the mouths of the proprietors of our modern luxury picture houses will water when they read of these high prices. The show was held in the town hall and was, of course, a huge success, the hall being packed even the standing room.

Some of my readers may laugh today at the old-time pictures that were resuscitated for us, to our huge delight, by the modern motion-picture companies. They will be interested to know that we saw that day for the first time, and were duly amazed at, facsimiles of the pictures at which we are roaring with merriment today! The famous 'pillow fight' was one of them, I remember. That was considered particularly wonderful for it was put on backwards, and all the feathers went back into the pillow cases. How we exclaimed at the marvels of this wonderful new invention!

The Rowing Club which had survived, or perhaps arisen from, the ashes of the long defunct Yacht Club, was in a fairly flourishing condition when I joined it soon after coming out. Its headquarters were along the Singapore River, where the Marine Police Station is today. It possessed six usable boats, two four-oars, two pairs and two sculling shells. I seemed to be fairly successful on the sliding seat—though I had never done anything but heavy sea rowing up till the day of my arrival—for I rowed fairly regularly in the various races, either at two or three. In the Annual Regatta I rowed with Scoular as stroke, and the others in the boat were fellows named Lane and Emerson, both long since gone from the place.

We did well in this regatta, it seems, because I have a mug with the date 1901 on it, though I cannot, at this time, remember the details of the event.

Sometimes we suffered casualties. On certain days it was very difficult to get the frail craft out of the mouth of the river, and great care had to be exercised. It was the custom to row across the front to the calm water in the mouth of the Kallang River, but occasionally we never got that far. One one occasion I distinctly recall sinking exactly opposite the centre of the esplanade, and having to swim and wade ashore in the mud in full view of all the female beauties that used to sit in their carriages and take the air on the esplanade every afternoon. A most inglorious return to land.

We made an attempt to form a minstrel troupe towards the end of the year. I do not remember that it ever came to anything much, but we got so far as to give ourselves a name, The City Minstrels, and to call a first rehearsal. I think one performance was given. The only other minstrel troupe that I remember was the one that attended the opening of the 'new' swimming club, but more of that in its proper place.

It is interesting to note that the children's concerts, which I resuscitated successfully some two years ago, were running merrily in 1901, and that the procedure adopted then was practically the same as it is now. The Philharmonic Orchestra usually played at these events. They were not run by the society but by Major St Clair himself. Tickets were sent out to schools, as is done today, and adults were admitted upon payment of S$1, the same sum that they are asked to pay now and for the same reason: to help pay the expenses of printing and advertising.

On the August bank holiday weekend of 1901, I made my first trip to Johore.

And you, good people, who get into your cars and drive backwards and forwards to Johore over the causeway in about forty-five minutes, shall hear about that trip and learn how we used to amuse ourselves in those old days.

We cycled!

Erny Abrams, a son of Daddy, the horse dealer, was in our firm, and together we arranged to spend our weekend holiday in Johore. Neither of us had bicycles at the time so we hired them, along with two bags to fasten to the frame and carry our clothes in. At five o'clock we set out from The Castle, Cavenagh Road, Abrams' home. We got to Bukit Timah village without any incident. I have before me the account of that trip that I wrote at the time to my parents at home, and I cannot do better than quote from it, as it gives a lively description of the countryside in those days. Referring to Bukit Timah—where the road was much higher and steeper than it is today, having been cut away time and again—I wrote:

'It is a lovely rise through a beautifully wooded country, and as the sun had, by this time, gone down, the temperature was not too great. But when I had worked my way up the last bit of the hill I was done for. Not being used to cycling, it was all I could do to get up it.

'However, we got to the top and there called a halt to blow up tyres and get a breather ourselves. And there we watched a pitched battle between red and black ants, a most interesting sight. The "reds" came in armies from one bank, the "blacks" from another. The opposing forces met in the middle of the red laterite road and a tremendous fight took place. We watched, fascinated, for a long time until the fading light warned us that we must push on, so we got on our machines and freewheeled merrily down the hill.

'We were now entering the jungle proper which was very thick, and the road wound a good deal. It was a lovely evening; the sun was setting over the trees away in front of us and night was rapidly closing in. We rushed through a native village in a small clearing (probably Bukit Panjang), getting up extra speed to escape the pariah dogs, the bane of the cyclist as they take a special delight in snapping at riders' calves.

'Leaving this hamlet behind, we entered upon the first stage of the run through the jungle to Kranji. This was really the most magnificent, though not perhaps the safest, part of the ride and as we saw it just as night was drawing in, it was lovely but rather eerie. It is here that tigers can be met with, and Erny enlivened the ride by telling me how, some short while back, he had driven with his father to Johore and about here met the Sultan of Johore with his trackers. It appeared that a tiger had sprung out of the jungle at the side of a road, killed a man in charge of a small roadroller and carried off the bullock that was drawing it! Just as Abrams told me this we passed the identical roller, derelict, at the roadside! It was now quite dark, and I don't think I am exaggerating at all when I say that from then until we saw the lights of Kranji ahead, we beat our records for speed! Tiger stories are all very well, but they should not be told in the dark in the identical spot where the incident took place!

'We left our bicycles at Kranji Police Station, and took a sampan over to Johore. On the way we passed close to a big log of wood which, as we passed, flicked a tail and disappeared! It was a big alligator. In those days the Straits were full of them. We landed in the mud at Johore as the tide was low but finally, at about eight o'clock, found ourselves in the rest house, then managed by a Mr Gawler (afterwards Dato Gawler), a very old and respected resident of Johore.

'Next day we "did" Johore. It was different then from what it is today. Gambling was permitted, and we tried our hands at the various native games and lost some money—but not too much. We went past the jail and saw the gangs of prisoners, in chains, working on the roads. We went to the sultan's Ladies' Bathing Pagar—Gawler having obtained the key for us—and had a swim. We went and saw the sultan's tigers that were kept in big cages outside the prison, and we met the sultan's ADC, Captain Daud, who said the sultan was going after a tiger next morning and would be pleased if we would go with him. Needless to say, we declined with thanks. We met the sultan himself the next day for he called in at the rest house on his way to his hunt.

'We left Johore in a sampan for Kranji on the Monday, after tiffin, and after cycling for about a mile and a half, my tyre burst! There was nothing for it but to ride on the rim, which I did until Bukit Panjang was reached. There we found rickshaws, so I put my bicycle in one, myself in another and set off home.'

The account I wrote at the time goes into detail about that ride, but it is sufficient here to say that we left the village at twenty past six in the evening, and I was home at Zetland House at a quarter past seven, having done the journey of over eleven miles, including the climb up the hill at Bukit Timah, in five minutes under the hour, without changing rickshaws or pullers! Believe me, pullers *were* pullers in those days.

On 21 October of this year, there occurred a rickshaw strike; in point of fact, it was the last one that was to ever seriously upset the even tenor of Singapore's transport problem and it is, therefore, of more than ordinary interest, and worthy of being recounted in some detail.

The strike was well arranged and complete. With the exception of a few private rickshaws, there were none on the streets at all. Residents these days can hardly understand what this meant to the inhabitants thirty years ago. I suppose that then seventy-five percent of the Europeans used rickshaws to get back and forth to the office, and for the Eurasians and other portions of the populace rickshaws were almost the only means of transport.

Private carriages and public gharries—the latter expensive—were the only other methods before trams and buses came in.

The day the strike occurred was windy with patches of rain. The mail was in that morning, and the offices had to be reached somehow. There was nothing to be done but to 'hoof' it. So away went the male portion of the population, carrying Chinese umbrellas and the inevitable tiffin basket, hoping against hope that someone would pass in a horse-drawn vehicle and give them a lift.

Imagine it, you who roll easily to your office today in your saloon cars. Imagine your predecessors trudging along Orchard and Grange Roads, their white boots covered with the red mud of a wet laterite road—a mud which stained!—and send a little prayer of thanks to Mr Austin and Mr Morris and their friends who have delivered you forever from such experiences as we had then! Happy was the man who owned a bicycle on that day of the strike.

The origin of the strike seems to have been a demand from the police that the men who pulled rickshaws should know something of the rules of the road. The governor had had occasion a few months before to report one who had run into his trap, nearly causing an accident, and when the police made their reasonable demand it was immediately concluded by the ignorant men that the governor was out for blood. Actually the police were right, for when Mr Hooper, the head of the jinricksha department, summoned a meeting of rickshaw *towkay*, about 150 turned up but only two had acquired copies of the rickshaw regulations which, printed in Chinese, were at their disposal.

At the close of the meeting, the idea of needing more order had penetrated the brains of those foolish owners to such a small extent that they went away and told the pullers that the police were going to fine them $5 a head—an obvious lie. So the strike began with the rowdy element threatening to smash the rickshaws of the more peaceful men if they didn't join in.

Unfortunately the matter did not end with the mere strike, and numerous instances of people on bicycles being pelted with missiles and pedestrians assaulted were reported, so much so that police officers were ordered to carry revolvers, and many of the other ranks were armed in some way or another.

The strike spread to the gharry-wallahs who were frightened to go on the streets for fear of being attacked, and as the day wore on, the situation worsened. Word went round that the Europeans would be advised to arm themselves, too. John Little and Robinsons were besieged with anxious purchasers of small arms, and that day I purchased my first—and last—revolver. Whether these instructions came from the authorities or not I do not know, but it is quite certain that we were not prevented from carrying revolvers if we had them.

That night things got very dangerous. Two or three of us escorted some ladies from Zetland House to their home in River Valley Road, with our loaded revolvers in our hands. We then made our way to the end of Coleman Street to have a look at the esplanade, which was like Hyde Park on a Sunday afternoon except that the moon was the only light available. Rather a weird scene, that big open space crowded with excited crowds of Chinese.

The principal roads were well guarded with armed police and police reserves were standing by at various central spots, but the night wore away without any serious trouble.

The morning broke gloomily and soon the rain came down in torrents, but the coolies absolutely refused to work so we had to trudge dismally to the office again.

That day there were some ugly scenes, and in Chinatown the police had to make arrests and shots were fired in the air to frighten the crowds. Along Rochor Road and in the district round the rickshaw station, the strikers were active and considerable damage was done.

The governor then took a very firm attitude and summoned the *towkay* to attend Government House. He explained to them that they were on British soil, and what they could do in China they could not practise here with impunity.

The actual events at that meeting are not known, the newspapers rather contradicting themselves when reporting it. But the rumours, whether actually true or not, were generally accepted at the time.

It was said that His Excellency kept the *towkay* waiting at Government House for about an hour, sending in biscuits and drinks to them. When he did appear he talked to them affably about the weather etc. and said it was very nice of them to call and see him. After a short while he excused himself, saying that he was very busy, and just as he was leaving the room he turned to them and said: 'Oh, by the by, gentlemen, there's a rickshaw strike on in town. There's also a boat leaving for China tomorrow. If that strike is not stopped before the ship leaves, you'll be on it! Good morning.'

Whether this actually happened or not I cannot say, but certain it is that the next day the strike was called off, and in a few hours the vehicles were out on the streets again and Singapore quickly resumed its normal aspect.

Some curious repercussions of the strike kept cropping up, however, from time to time.

One Sunday night I went to dinner at the residence of the Salzmanns as usual, and a sister from the hospital was there, too, and I offered to escort her home. We left the Salzmanns' house in St Thomas' Walk in rickshaws, and when we came to the junction of Kim Seng and River Valley Roads and made to turn down the former, the pullers put down the shafts and refused to budge. No amount of argument would get them to do down Kim Seng Road, and eventually I worked out the reason. It was that the governor had offered a price of S$100 for the head of a rickshaw coolie cut off in that thoroughfare! And so we had to walk, and an eerie and evil-smelling walk it was! No lamps and swamp on either side until we got to Havelock Road, where we got another rickshaw. I went home from the hospital another way!

For some time the Wynters, who were the leading dramatic spirits in the place, had been making preparations for another show and I had been chosen to take part.

Captain Wynter with whom I was, by this time, very friendly

had learnt that my principal line was comic opera, and was very anxious to introduce me to a Singapore audience in a role where my voice could be used. So he prefaced his choice of *Charley's Aunt* with a little operetta called *Grass Widows*, quite a frothy little play as regards plot but with nice music. Mrs Wynter, a Mrs Pickering and myself were to act in it, and also in *Charley's Aunt* afterwards.

The performances duly came off and were a great success. It seems it was quite an experience for Singapore to find a new actor, for the papers were very kind to me, remarking upon the fact that I seemed to know the value of 'keeping still' as a stage accomplishment, and called my singing and acting 'much above the ordinary amateur level'.

Looking back after a long lapse of years on these shows of ours, and comparing them with the elaborate and almost London-like productions that I have produced during the last decade, I often wonder what the talent really *was* like then! I suppose very much the same as it is now, but the facilities available for amateurs are so far ahead of what they were then, that we may *seem* much better today.

A funny incident occurred during the performance of *Charley's Aunt*. The day before the last performance, Jules Fabris, who was playing the 'aunt', was bitten in the calf by a dog. A special rehearsal was hurriedly called; Wynter, who was playing Jack Chesney, took over Fabris' part; I, who was playing Charley Wyckham, took on Wynter's part and the prompter, Georgie Greig, was roped in to play my part. And all at twenty-four hours' notice! It was exceedingly funny to watch Wynter, who stood over six foot, trying to make himself small enough to fit the part of Charley's aunt.

The play was such a success that we had to extend the season, and the original three nights ran into six before the run finally came to an end, the last performance being in aid of the building fund of the Recreation Club.

In November 1901 the offer of the Straits Chinese to provide a volunteer company for the Settlement was accepted by the secretary of state 'with much appreciation', and the company duly came into being. It was with this company that a great part of my Volunteer service was to be spent, and it is interesting to note that my right-hand man all through the busy and strenuous times of the Great War was Captain Song Ong Siang, the original recruiter for the company.

On 21 November 1901 Sir Arthur Sullivan died. On 26 November 1901 the Singapore Philharmonic Society remembered the death of one of England's greatest musicians in a memorial concert in the town hall. At that concert I sang 'The Highland Message' or, as it is more often called, 'Thou'rt Passing Hence, My Brother'. It had been orchestrated for the occasion by Major St Clair, and the newspapers of the day paid me the compliment of writing: 'A great song, finely sung.'

5

1902

The beginning of this year found me still living at Zetland House with the Whitefields. I had, by now, quite settled down to my new life, had made plenty of friends and was receiving my full share of invitations to the houses of the Tuan Besars. I had been admitted to the Ladies' Lawn Tennis Club as a subscriber, and that in itself was a ticket of eligibility because the committee consisted of ladies only, and the club was, as a consequence, very difficult to get into. It sounds funny in these democratic days to write this, but it is a fact that, at that time, to be able to call oneself 'of the Ladies' Lawn' was a definite statement of the fact that one had 'arrived'. I have a shrewd suspicion, however, that my real passport lay in my voice for there had not been a trained baritone in Singapore for some years and Robert Dunman, who was a full bass, was far past his prime when I came to Singapore.

Early in January of this year the Singapore Volunteer Engineers were raised 'to assist the Royal Engineers in the permanent defence of the colony'. The company was to be divided into two sections, Field and Electrical, and enlistment in either section was optional. Present-day Volunteers will be interested to learn that one of the incentives to join up was 'a hundred rounds of ammunition free and a hundred at half price'.

In January I took part in a concert given by Herr and Madame Marquardt. These two were well-known professionals in their day, the former being a violinist of no mean order and the latter a performer on that rare but beautiful instrument, the harp. It is worth while mentioning this concert because I think it was the last time the harp was heard in Singapore until this year (1933) that I am writing in. A few months ago, however, I had a visitor at my office in the shape of a young American lady who was passing through and who thought of giving a concert. When I heard that she was a harpist, I engaged her there and then to play at a children's concert that same afternoon, and at the end of the programme the harp was put at the edge of the platform, and the whole audience of about 800 children filed past to get a closer view of this strange and wonderful instrument that none of them had ever heard or seen before.

At the Marquardts' concert I sang Wolfram's song from *Tannhäuser*, 'O Star of Eve', and also did a duet with Mrs Salzmann. The copies of this duet were sent to me a short while ago by Mrs Salzmann 'in memory of old times' just before she left Singapore for good. Ambrose Cross was at the piano throughout the evening as accompanist; if he ever reads this he will probably recollect the occasion.

The Town and Volunteer Band was now in existence and was well received. Its place of performance was on the esplanade. The honour of playing 'in the gardens' was reserved for the combined bands of the 3rd and 13th Madras Infantry, which were then stationed here. There was no regular battalion of white troops here—the South African War was still keeping the home army busy.

Early in this year admiral of the fleet, Sir Harry Keppel, arrived in Singapore on a visit to his old friend, Mr C.B. Buckley. I had the honour of meeting him and looking after him—for he was very frail—at a children's party that C.B. was giving. I helped him to his seat and sat with him. He was, I think, one of the smallest men I have ever met, but in spite of this age and frailty I was impressed by his fine face. He was born on 7 February 1819 so was eighty-three years of age when I met him, and his first visit to Singapore was on 5 September 1832! What changes the old man must have seen when he came back to his old 'hunting ground' in the early part of this present century. He had then lived under no less than five sovereigns of England, having been born in the reign of George III. I suppose I am now the last European in Singapore who has ever met and spoken with him.

His photo had been presented to Singapore and hung in the old town hall in August 1901.

Plans for raising the funds for the memorial to Queen Victoria were, by this time, in motion, and on 31 January a meeting was held at which representatives of all nationalities were chosen to canvass their respective peoples. It was stated at the meeting that Sir Frank Swettenham was opening the subscription list with a donation of S$1,000.

On Wednesday, 5 February the Singapore Volunteer Corps went into camp. Much was written of this camp at the time, known for years as The Wet Camp, and several of the more interesting incidents are recorded elsewhere under the heading, 'The Bad Old Days'. It was a camp of mistakes. Everything, from the weather downwards, seemed to go wrong. I was in a tent with Darbyshire, afterwards an MP; Billings, who was living with the Whitefields at the time and who afterwards became headmaster of the Shanghai Public School; a fellow called Hankin, rather a rolling stone who had just joined up, and had been a war correspondent for a New York paper during the late troubles in China, and had, I believe, been one of the first of the relieving force to enter Pekin; and the notorious Fargie, who was in Paterson, Simons & Co. Fargie's notoriety was born in this camp, as will be seen from the 'camp memories' already referred to.

We were, I am afraid, a most unruly crowd, and discipline in camp was very lax. Most of the rank and file knew more about their job than the officers did, I am afraid. One of the minor incidents I took part in was a night attack on the camp itself. The SVR were the attacking party, and I do not know to this day who the defenders were—they may have forgotten to appoint any! Be that as it may, we never saw them, and in the end the gang I was with found itself back in camp, and at the rear of the officers' mess tent.

Colonel Murray had a 'guest night', so we decided to finish our work in style and capture the dinner party! I can remember now the surprise and anger of Murray, and the delight of the guests, when the room was invaded by a party of men covered in mud from head to foot, with rifles in their hands, who forced the diners to leave their table and to stand in a row while their names were taken and they were told that they were under arrest!

We got it in the neck for that escapade, but not seriously because we all knew well enough that the colonel should have been out on the job and not showing off to his civilian friends. Nor had there been anything in the 'orders' to say that the officers' mess was not to be considered part of the camp for this occasion!

Billings, who was in charge of our tent number nine, wrote a long account of the camp to *The Straits Times*. It was written—and well written—in a humorous vein, but he got into trouble for it because he dared to poke fun at the colonel. He wrote of a certain field day that: 'A thrill went through the ranks when it was known that the occasion was of such gravity as to require the CO to be present, and that he would actually take part and be, as it were, for a time, one of us, the SVC.'

Result: a court martial for Billings. I think the whole of our tent were court martialled at some time or another during our stay at that camp!

I managed to get my own back, however. We were rehearsing some play at the time, and both Colonel Murray and I were in it, I assisting Captain Wynter with the production. It was very sweet to be able, from my position of stage manager, to tick the colonel off at night in return for the tickings off I had received during the day! He had to drive me up to town and back from the rehearsals in his dog cart, which added insult to injury!

On 13 February I took part in a complimentary benefit concert organised by friends for the Salzmanns. I sang the bass solos in a selection from *Eli* and, in the second part, a song that had become a great favourite—F. Aylward's 'Song of the Bow'. I had brought this song out to Singapore, and made it known in the place. The newspapers said on this occasion that I sang it with 'the same life and power which had won many encores for it in Singapore'. It remained a favourite for many years, right down to the end of the Great War. Sir Arthur Young, who had 'no music in his soul', would always stay in his drawing room until he heard whether Brown had brought The Bow, as he called it. If I had, he would wait. If I had not, he would go downstairs and play snooker!

I was now becoming known as a 'soccer' player. My real place on the field was goalkeeper, which I had occupied at school and afterwards in club football.

In those days they had a happy way of putting a player in a place he was totally unfit for and, being a goalkeeper, I got my first chance at halfback! I think I lasted about ten minutes in that first match. However, I was now playing fairly regularly at left fullback, Billings being in goal. A fine goalkeeper he was, too. The only other one of that old team that is now left is Farrer, who was one of the nippiest outsides in the forward line that we ever had.

One of the biggest fires I have ever seen in Singapore occurred early in March this year. The trouble started on the north bank of the river, just by Kim Seng Bridge where there were, at that time, a lot of boat builders. A strong breeze was blowing from the north-east and the flames quickly spread.

I was in the Cricket Club that afternoon and was talking to a Mr Wathen, the acting CPO. Someone came in and said that there seemed to be a fire up River Valley Road way. Wathen told me to come along if I cared to, so I jumped into his gig and away we went. When we got to Havelock Road Police Station the sparks, fanned by the strong breeze, were blowing right across the river. There was a real danger that the Malay huts which then lined the banks by the bridge would catch fire. There was no fire brigade to be seen—it was probably the other side of the river—so we set to work to demolish the Malay huts as quickly as possible. Malay constables were pushed up onto the roofs, and the attaps were torn down as quickly as could be, but all to no purpose, for the sparks caught a house and in a minute the whole place was ablaze. Both sides of the river were now well alight for hundreds of yards; native houses, *tongkang*, stacks of timber, boats on the stocks, pig yards, everything was gobbled up by the flames. The air was full of the squealing of pigs for many of them, poor brutes, were in their baskets and were being roasted alive. The river was full of escaping animals, and the smell of roast pork went all over the town. Huttenbach's godown was in danger for a time but the fire brigade, which had now come to the south side of the river, concentrated on the building and saved it, though it was actually on fire at one corner.

The flames rose to a tremendous height and could be seen all over Singapore, and it really was a very fine and awesome sight. The water brilliantly reflected the flames that were blazing on both sides of the river and the heat was, of course, tremendous.

Astonishingly little insurance money was involved; including the damage to Huttenbach's godown, the loss was only about

S$30,000, and a great deal of good was done in clearing up a portion of the river bank that had been a standing disgrace to the hygienic conditions of the town for some years.

As usual, the poor old fire brigade came in for some nasty knocks; it was alleged that the hose was so leaky that more water went out of the sides than came out in the jet, and only in fits and starts could the stream be made to reach to the roof of the godowns! Over twelve months had elapsed since the committee of enquiry had been formed; the report had been prepared and handed in months before but the municipality had done nothing! The newspapers printed numerous letters from eyewitnesses which proved conclusively that the allegations were true. I think it was this fire that finally forced the municipality to get a move on and start the reorganisation of their totally inadequate fire brigade.

It is interesting to note that at about this time Singapore heard its first pianola, and was greatly surprised thereat. First the bioscope and then the pianola, and in places nearer the hub of the world there were whispers of a wonderful thing called wireless telegraphy! A fellow called Marconi had sat on a yacht out at sea and had received telegraphic messages from the shore without any telegraph wires being fixed! What a wonderful world we lived in then, to be sure! People who wished to be thought clever used to prophesy that magic lantern pictures would soon be made to talk to us! Funny fellows!

Well, well, it's a funny world and you never can tell. I discovered once among some family papers a diary, written by my great-grandfather, of a trip from Holyhead to Dublin by the first steamboat that crossed! He had gone specially on the trip, and had written his experiences down because, as he said in a foreword to the diary, he wanted his children's children to know something about this new and wonderful thing that had come to the world. However, it was felt it would only be a fad of a day or so as it was not expected to last, not being possible as a commercial proposition!

And, just as I write, a letter has been brought from Amsterdam to Batavia by air in four and a half days! Heigh ho!

But I am wandering ...

All the talk now was of the coming coronation of King Edward, and Singapore was delighted when a telegram from the secretary of state instructed that the Straits Settlements should be represented by fifty Volunteers, and the Malay States by fifty of the Malay States Guides. I badly wanted to go with the Singapore contingent as, I suppose, did every other Volunteer, but leave for me was not due or near due, and the people who went were either men due for leave or servants of the government or municipality who could be more easily spared.

In the end Chinese, Eurasian and European Volunteers were represented, and among the first named were those afterwards distinguished citizens of Singapore—Dr Lim Boon Keng and Mr Song Ong Siang. Both these gentlemen had been Queen's Scholars from Raffles School, and both were to rise later to high honours in the colony. In fact Dr Lim Boon Keng was, even at that time, a member of the Legislative Council.

We played a triple bill on Friday, 21 March and succeeding

nights to mark the departure from our midst of Captain Wynter and his charming wife. The Wynters had been the life and soul of amateur dramatics during their stay here, and it was with genuine sorrow that we parted with them. The triple bill consisted of *Sunset*, by Jerome; a musical play, *The Crusader and the Craven*, in which Mrs Wynter, Lionel Koek and myself took part; and that old favourite, *The Pantomime Rehearsal*, in which Wynter played while I 'stage-managed'—my first attempt at production.

I do not remember much about the show, except that we had discovered a new and charming actress in the person of Mrs Whitehead, wife of a police officer. In order to get her we had to give a part to her husband, who was not much good but who caused much amusement among the players by shaving off a perfectly good moustache in order, I suppose, to look like an actor, and then fixing a false one for the play the exact facsimile of the one he had shaved off! *The Crusader and the Craven* was a bad choice, having no plot and poor music. *Pantomime Rehearsal* was very much what it was meant to be, I'm afraid. I played the small part of Tomkins and, as I have said, produced it.

The Wynters left by the German mail steamer, *Kiautschou*, on 24 March, and were presented on departure with a silver salver to commemorate the hard work they had put into amateur dramatics and as a token of remembrance from their many friends. I never met or heard of them again until the Great War broke out, when I saw poor Wynter's name and the word 'killed' in almost the first list of casualties that came through.

Presentations were in the air at this time. Major St Clair had been presented by the governor, at a recent Philharmonic concert, with a gold watch and chain as a return for his services to music, and his office was invaded on 2 April by a body of gentlemen who handed him a 'handsome conductor's baton' and an illuminated address! They don't do this kind of thing nowadays.

How would present-day residents like to meet a tiger in town? And yet there was one, about this time, in the Bukit Timah Road cemetery at the bottom of Cavenagh Road. Sergeant Keyworth, a well-known Volunteer who was employed in the water department, took his gun and followed the spoor until he lost it in a bit of jungle nearby. He came to the conclusion that it was a panther and not a tiger, which made matters worse. It does not seem to have been caught, however.

On Thursday, 10 April a horrible murder, resulting in the death of Mr Rutherford, Managing Director of the Tanjong Pagar Dock Company, was committed at a house called Draycott. Mr Rutherford's niece, a Miss Gunn, was also seriously wounded. This lady is now Lady Penny, wife of the Rt Hon. Sir George Penny, Bart., MP. It is unnecessary to go into the details here, but it caused a tremendous outcry at the time and was the sequel to a long list of burglaries that had taken place in Tanglin and the district during the preceding few months.

There was money in show business in those days. People who remember the old Dallas Company—afterwards the Bandman Company—can recall the enthusiasm that used to greet the arrival of this band of players who toured the East with such success. It did not matter much what they played or how they played it—I have seen a new play given out to the company on the train after leaving Ipoh, which was produced in Singapore within forty-eight hours—they were always certain of crowded houses and an enthusiastic welcome. Many people afterwards famous on the stage passed through the hands of old Henry Dallas. One of them, Frith, is now 'big noise' in the theatrical world in Australia. I believe he was a trooper in the Dragoon Guards originally, and joined the Dallas Company in Calcutta. Anyhow, he was a wonderful actor and excruciatingly funny.

I used to know the company well, and was always welcomed behind the scenes. In those days it did not matter much if the company was an hour or so late in starting. Everyone was very kind to the professionals, and made allowances for every mistake. We had paid to have an evening's enjoyment and we were determined to get value for our money. How different things are nowadays. Fifty percent of an audience today will compare a show with 'what they saw in London' and go and tell their friends that the performance is no good because it does not come up to the London standard! It was much easier to amuse people in the old days and Singapore—and other places in the East—have largely themselves to thank for the dearth of theatrical performances, both professional and amateur, nowadays.

Another distinguished professional I met about this time was Mr Alec Marsh, for years the leading bass in the Carl Rosa Opera Company and one of the finest Mephistopheles that England ever produced. He had been touring the East and was on his way home. Like all of his kind he found his way to Zetland House, and he, I and Ambrose Cross had one or two fine evenings together. Some of my more ambitious songs are still marked with his pencil where he was good enough to give me tips in the rendering of them. He was, of course, past his prime when I met him, but was even then a great singer.

By special request he turned up at the farewell 'smoker' to the coronation contingent held in the drill hall on 25 April and kindly sang a couple of songs.

While he was here some fellows arranged a launch picnic for him at Raffles Light. Seeing the coconut palms there he expressed a wish to taste the milk of a nut. One was procured and, on the pretence of having it opened, was taken out of sight and filled up with neat gin! It was then brought to Alec Marsh, and the conspirators stood around waiting for the successful end to their little trick. Imagine their surprise when Alec Marsh drank the whole of the contents without turning a hair, smacked his lips and asked for another!

At the end of May I was at last back in my proper position on the football field, and was playing in goal for the club in cup-tie matches. There were three or four teams only in those days, no natives played at all. The three were the SCC, the RE and one or two teams from the RGA—it depended on the number of companies in garrison. The matches for the cup used to attract an enormous amount of interest even then, and the gambling that used to go on around the goalposts among the Malay spectators was most amusing to listen to.

The Second Boer War ended officially on 31 May and on

Monday, 2 June the telegrams reported that the terms of surrender had been accepted and signed by the Boer representatives, Lord Kitchener and Lord Milner.

So ended a war which had started on 11 October 1899, had run on for two years and seven months, and had had singularly little effect upon the lives and habits and customs of these parts. The day was to come when a war would break out that would bring the fighting and the horrible toll of war to our very doors, but we were not to know this, and we duly shut our offices and rejoiced with the Empire that the Second Boer War was over.

Early in June a new travelling company came to the theatre, the Barnes Company. They are of little interest to me now, and I should have forgotten all about them if it had not been for the fact that they brought with them as their soprano a lady who called herself Madame Agnes Freed. She was billed as The Californian Nightingale. She was certainly Californian and she had a voice, but neither she nor her voice looked or sounded like a nightingale! I mention the fact now because I shall have more to say about her later on.

The coronation day of King Edward was now approaching. The Volunteer contingents from the East had sailed, and there was bustle and preparation in Singapore for the proper celebration of the great event. C.B. Buckley, The Children's Friend (can a man have a greater name than that?), had been to the committee and announced that he was going to get up a show for the children which would be something they would remember all their lives. In due course a big notice appeared in the papers, and placards were posted about the town which announced in quaint language that Ye Coronation Fayre was to be held.

In the method of the announcements of the old English fairs, it started with:

'OYEZ, OYEZ, OYEZ
ON WODEN-HYS-DAYE YE 25 JUNE
There shall be holden at ye houre of 4.30 by
ye clok in ye afternoone, on ye great space of
grounde in front of Raffles Hys Inne,
weather permittynge
YE CORONATION FAYRE'

and it went on to set forth the attractions of the fair:

'A Tunefulle Bande of Musicianers
Master Richardson Hys Booke
A Thryllinge Drama of Mysterie
Tradedie and Villianie yclept
'Bleede for Bleede'
Ye Lanterne
Ye Magician
lykewyse
Ye Buxom Ladye
Ye Fortune Tellers
Ye Stronge Manne
Ye Craftie Wizard'

They were all there and, needless to say, we were all going to be there too, for Buckley had roped in all the lads of the village who could do anything at all in the line of entertainment and, of course, everyone was only too willing to help. It looked like being a great show, and we spent our spare time perfecting our parts, arranging for our costumes and waiting for the day.

There had been, for some time, a movement on foot to form a cadet corps at the schools. It had received the sanction of the government, but there had been a lot of acrimonious correspondence about it. It was pointed out that the war was over and the world—that is, the British world which was now considerably larger than three years before—was settling down to peace again. Yet here was the rascally government intent on training the youth to be soldiers. Allegations were also put forward to the effect that the corps would be a sort of conscript class for the Volunteers, and that when a boy left school he would be 'drafted' into the SVC whether he liked it or not!

However, the movement was passed, and various entertainments were arranged to provide the funds for equipping the boys. On 20 June a performance took place at the theatre, during the course of which I produced my first Sullivan opera, *Cox and Box*. I almost wrote 'Gilbert and Sullivan' but, of course, Gilbert was to come later; the words of *Cox and Box* are by F.C. Burnand. A fellow called Long, on the *Singapore Free Press* staff, played Cox, I played Box and that genial Singaporean and good fellow Noel Skey—then a young man—had the part of Sergeant Bouncer.

If I remember rightly it was not a very good show, but the papers were very kind to us and told us that we sang 'Sullivan's none too easy music' with great success! The papers were really nice to amateurs in those days!

Anyhow, we raised a substantial sum for the Cadets, so all was well.

Buckley's show was now the talk of the town. It was to be a Children's Show, pure and simple, and tickets for grown-ups were very difficult to get. If you were rich and had subscribed S$25, Buckley allowed you *one* ticket. And the only way you could get another was to subscribe another S$25. Buckley, when he made a rule, stuck to it.

Rumour had it that 5,000 to 6,000 children would be present; that 13,000 buns had been ordered in one order; that sandwiches were to be cut by an army of ladies and gentlemen from daybreak until one o'clock; that the Fat Lady was getting thin through nervousness and was being fattened up with Easton's Syrup and, in fact, that preparations were being pushed forward 'on a scale of unparalleled magnificence, prodigality and profusion'. We knew the use of high-sounding words in those days, yes, and used 'em, too!

And then, flop! On the morning of the great day the telegrams came through: THE KING ILL—CORONATION POSTPONED. What were we to do? All preparations made, everything ready for the great show, and then the reason for it all was taken away. There would be no coronation!

Buckley did the only sensible thing. He persuaded the

committee that the spirit of the coronation was there, whether the actual event took place that day or later; that the children were all keyed up for the fun; that the same real happiness and jollity could never be manufactured again on another date—once gone it would never return—and that, anyhow, coronation in London or not, his Children's Show in honour of the King was going to go ahead and that was that!

As usual, when Buckley put his foot down no one dared to contradict (the only person who could do it with impunity was Mrs Salzmann), and word was passed round the town that the show was on and we must be at our appointed stations at the time arranged.

And what a wonderful afternoon it was. The weather was lovely, though there had been rain in the morning, and everyone was out to be as mad as possible and make the children happy. Less-inspired citizens—those of the S$25 pockets—may have walked about with long faces and exchanged such platitudes as 'What terrible news!', 'It has thrown a damper over everything,' 'Such a pity for the kiddies,' and kindred sentences, but they never made a bigger mistake in their lives. For the 'kiddies', from the real little toddlers to the synthetic kiddies who, in private life, were staid and sober businessmen, were there to enjoy themselves and be happy, and they succeeded beyond their dreams. The fun of it all! Even today, after over thirty years, I can still get a thrill when I cast my mind back and see again the picture of that old English fair and the crowds of laughing, excited children as they dashed from booth to booth and stall to stall; standing in little crowds around one 'silly ass' who was doing something funny on a table, until a louder laugh from nearby attracted their fickle attention and they rushed off, only to have their places taken by another crowd of open-mouthed kiddies.

Have you ever been in a position where there was *too much* entertainment? I once went to Barnum & Bailey's three-ringed circus and I know exactly the feelings of those children that afternoon!

And the noise! Banging of drums, blowing of trumpets, touts in all sorts of weird costumes bawling out the merits of their respective shows. No wonder the children felt that their parents should have arranged for them to have swivel necks; they simply could not turn their heads around fast enough.

And what of the fun-makers? Well, we were all there, working our hardest. Let us stroll round the place and see what is going on. We can leave the town band alone, also the newly formed SVI (Chinese Company) who, in their smart uniforms, slouch hats and swagger canes, were much in evidence 'keeping order'.

Here we are at the hub of things, 'Master Buckley, hys eerye.' A great platform erected in the centre of the ground, reached by a ladder. From this lookout Buckley could control his show with the aid of a megaphone and his eagle eye, the latter missing nothing.

Watch him! He's seen something! Down the ladder he comes, and with his black bowler (which he always wore) on the back of his head and his handkerchief in his mouth as usual, he tears off to one end or other of the show to put right something that hasn't satisfied him. Very often it is nothing but a poor tout outside a show who doesn't come up to what Buckley's idea of a tout should be.

Watch him seize the man's drum, push him off his stand and 'give him a lesson'. Poor, dear old Buckley! If ever a man managed to be in more than one place at one time, it was Buckley on that great day. And what a nuisance he was! All one's carefully rehearsed and thought-out quips and jokes were ruined if they didn't meet with his approval. Like a whirlwind he would come down on us, and we would presently find ourselves standing meekly like a naughty child among the crowd while C.B. stood up in our place and showed us 'how it ought to be done'.

But it was all in a day's work, all the fun of the fair, and no one minded. No one ever did take old Buckley amiss.

Here we are at the tent where scenes of blood and gore are repeated every hour. Let us go in and watch the children as they witness that heart-rending drama, *Blood for Blood*, written by A.B. Cross and first performed at Zetland House. A critic would have said that the 'orchestra' was the cleverest part because, throughout, Cross accompanied his play on the piano, making the music fit the crime, so to speak. As he extemporised the whole time and never once took his hands from the keys, it was really something worth remembering. Everyone on the stage died regularly, hour after hour, through that long hot afternoon and evening. It was a luvverly drrrama!

Come along, here's a comic donkey! Let's go in and see it. Ooh! They've got a headless man there, too!

And quick, run across to this booth, there's a fat woman here!

Poor Davis, I can't remember whether he was American Consul or Head of Standard Oil but he weighed well over eighteen stone and, for the good of the cause, had dressed himself up in a nice starched frock and sunbonnet, big blue sash, socks and ankle-strap shoes! What a sight he looked! And, of course, there was his opposite, the 'thin man', in the same booth.

In the next tent are the minstrels, fun by Coghlan, and including in their ranks such well-known names as Diss, Harry Noon, Keiller, Algy Langley and lots of others.

Here's a wizard. He seems to have his booth full always, for there's a funny clown at the door continually turning people away and telling them not to mind, they will find room somewhere else! Truly philanthropic were our touts on this day! And then there were funny men, performing their antics among the crowds, and lots of other shows.

And I? Oh, I was the quack doctor. I don't remember much about what I did, except that my costume was a *very* tall hat, a *very* long moustache and a kind of George Robey frock coat. And I remember that Jimmy McKenzie of the dispensary had 'fitted me out' with scores of bottles with harmless coloured water in. But I suppose I must have done my bit all right, for the paper of the day referred to, 'A doctor of the profoundest quackery who talked the drollest nonsense and diagnosed pneumonia in the boots of his patients, and equally abstruse and serious maladies.'

And when darkness came and we had to give up, we were all ready to drop. Raffles Hotel, the nearest 'pub', was invaded by the most awful collection of apparitions that possibly it had ever seen for, of course, everyone was wet through with exertion.

Unfortunately there was an anticlimax to the show. Buckley, in his exuberance, had decided to open at night for the general public and to have fireworks.

The fireworks were all right but, unfortunately, the lighting-up system which Buckley had arranged for would not work and, in addition, most of the sideshows' personnel went on strike, being completely done in after the strenuous efforts of the afternoon.

But it was a great day, and one to be remembered all one's life.

I learnt a lot of things that afternoon that stood me in good stead in later years when my turn came to organise and run bigger shows even than this was. I copied Buckley's idea of an 'eerie' for the Children's Corner when the Prince of Wales came to Singapore twenty years later, and my wife's Poppy Day Katong Park Fair was really based on Buckley's Children's Fête of 1902.

6

1902 (Continued)

In July the SCC Annual Sports was held. This meeting was quite a social event, and all the ladies turned out in their prettiest dresses. The programme was always very well supported. I carried off another mug this year, being one of the teams that won the five-a-side football competition. Sir Frank Swettenham, the governor, presented the prizes.

I was now playing in goal regularly for the club, Billings having left Singapore and gone to China. When I could not play my place was taken by C.W. Darbyshire and sometimes by George Penny.

The Town and Volunteer Band had, by this time, been moved from its pitch on the esplanade to the impounding reservoir at Mount Emily, where the municipal freshwater swimming pool is today. This was a place much frequented by *amahs* and children who lived in the neighbourhood, but I do not think the band attracted much outside attention. I think this was the last pitch before the band was disbanded; I do not remember the Volunteers using it after the regrettable incident mentioned in 'The Bad Old Days', though they still subscribed to its upkeep.

On 26 July a telegram was received by the governor to say that the coronation of the King, postponed on account of His

Majesty's illness, would take place on 9 August. Preparations were at once made to resuscitate all the festivities that had been lying dormant since the postponement. Saturday, 9 August and Monday, 11 August were declared public holidays, while the coronation ball at Government House was fixed for the twelfth. Practices of what was called the coronation choir and orchestra were resumed in the cathedral, and generally things began to liven up.

It is worthwhile recording here, in passing, that on 4 August 1902, the Tanjong Pagar Dock Company beat the world record in hand-coaling a ship, putting 1,548 tons of coal onto HMS *Terrible* on her homeward voyage. Work started at ten past seven in the morning, and by three in the afternoon only forty-eight tons remained to be put on board! The work then slackened off. Whereas 1,500 tons had been loaded in four hours and fifty three minutes, it took thirty-four minutes to get the remaining forty-eight tons on board.

To go back to the coronation. Decoration of the town was arranged. Ships were to be illuminated at night; there was to be a coronation ball in the town hall, and coronation dinners at the hotels; a coronation gymkhana, and in fact a coronation almost everything.

The official functions started with a parade of troops, and the accounts of this note that, 'In accordance with the new *Infantry Drill Book*, the men stood at ease in the latest approved fashion of feet wide apart, which gives a man a *helpless kind of look*, though it may be comfortable.'

I was not on that parade as it was followed immediately by the official service in the cathedral, and choirmen who were Volunteers were granted leave of absence from military duties. I don't remember much about that service, though I see from the papers that Buckley, who was still choirmaster, had arranged for a small orchestra to augment the organ.

What I *do* remember, however, is the parody that the choirmen insisted on singing during the anthem, 'Zadoc the Priest'.

The words are, of course, 'Zadoc the priest, and Nathan the prophet, anointed Solomon King.'

What we sang was: 'Izard the priest, and Nathan the broker, anointed Salzmann King.' Izard being at that time Colonial Chaplain, Malacca—he had been 'acting' in Singapore—Nathan being the Jew broker and opium magnate of Singapore, and Salzmann being our own organist!

Ribaldry, perhaps, but no one noticed the change of the words and we thought we were being funny, so everyone was satisfied!

Next came the laying of the foundation stone of the Victoria Memorial Hall, which was done by Sir Frank Swettenham, the governor. It was an official function and does not, therefore, require more than mention here.

For the rest of the day rejoicings of various kinds took place, and were continued far into the night. I suppose we all got to bed very much as others do today after similar celebrations. I see from the list of guests that I was present at the coronation ball at Government House, but I remember nothing at all about it.

A much more interesting event than official laying of

foundation stones etc. took place on 13 August and marked the end of the tiger stories of Singapore.

A tiger was shot under the billiard room of Raffles Hotel. To be sure it was one that had escaped from a show on Beach Road, but it had been free for some time and the night before had taken a walk to Johnston's Pier, boarded a *tongkang*, given a few friendly scratches to the Indian in charge, gone ashore again and disappeared. Very late that night a tremendous ado was caused in Raffles Hotel by Master Stripes peering through the low railing of the veranda at the boy in charge of the billiard room. The boy promptly took cover but, finding that nothing happened, he pulled himself together sufficiently to creep to a doorway and scoot.

This was at about midnight. In the early morning Stripes was located under the room, which was raised about four feet from the ground.

A message was sent across to Raffles School where the headmaster, Mr C.M. Phillips, at that time Singapore's crack rifle shot, was sleeping the sleep of the just—or the unjust—after a *very* late night at the ball at Government House. Charlie was not unnaturally annoyed at being awakened so early, and wanted to know what the hell was the matter. When things were explained to him he seemed to think that the tiger was responsible for his bad head, so he took his Enfield rifle and some cartridges and, clad only in his pyjamas, proceeded to the scene of action. The tiger was still under the billiard room, there was no doubt about that, yet no amount of peering into the gloom could discern his presence. Suddenly Charlie saw him and plunked three shots in quick succession into him. But no! There was some mistake. He didn't move. It must have been that Government House whisky again, for Charlie found he had fired at one of the brick supports of the building. By this time the tiger must have been as much fed up with Phillips as Charlie was, for he lay doggo and for a long time nothing could be seen. At last Phillips saw his eyes gleaming in the dark, and that was sufficient. A well-directed shot took the tiger in the spot between those gleaming eyes. Master Stripes had killed the tiger which was duly dragged out dead from its hiding place, to the intense joy of those people who had come home later than they should have done the night before, and had imagined that they had been seeing things! Now they had a real cast-iron excuse.

The most annoyed man of the lot was Charlie Phillips, who spoilt a perfectly good suit of pyjamas.

But if anyone wakes me up after a late night at Government House and tells me that there's a tiger about, I'm going to tell him that he's out of date, for Charlie Phillips shot that tiger on Wednesday, 13 August 1902!

About the middle of this year, the condition of the Singapore Volunteer Rifles began to cause anxiety. No recruits seemed to be forthcoming and, at a much later date, men said that the war was over and there was no need for further military training. Those that were in the corps began to neglect the drills, and the matter became so serious that at the corps Annual Meeting, a member got up and moved that a committee of enquiry be formed to enquire into the state of affairs. He was promptly snubbed by his colonel, the chairman, who told him that it was a matter for the corps officers to deal with. We certainly were not given much chance to allow our enthusiasm for volunteering to run riot! Anyhow, the officers did not succeed in doing anything and the death of the SVR was only a matter of time.

On 1 September there appeared a short notice in the papers to the effect that *HMS Pinafore*, which had been in rehearsal for some time, would be produced on 11 November. These rehearsals had not been without incident. The Wynters, prime movers in things dramatic, had gone home and left no enthusiast in their place. A lot of new and young talent was arriving but no use was being made of it. Up till the time of my first appearance, dramatic effort had been more or less a closed corner, with the same gang being picked every time. However, my début seemed to have awakened people to the fact that there must be just as good, or even better, talent among the young folks.

Finally some of those interested determined to see what could be done, and W.A. Dowley of Vacuum Oil, Peter Edlin of Drew & Napier, F.W. (Tubby) Barker and others got together and decided to produce a Gilbert and Sullivan opera. Mr Salzmann was engaged to do the musical part. Unfortunately there was no soprano in the place capable of singing Josephine, so Madame Freed, The Californian Nightingale, was engaged to stay in Singapore and play the part. (I think the company she had been with had gone bust in the Native States or somewhere. Singapore, in those days and for long afterwards, had the unenviable name in the profession of The Actor's Grave.)

Now The Freed, as we called her, could certainly sing—that is to say, she had a voice—but she couldn't act, and possessed no particle whatever of the G & S spirit. She simply didn't fit at all. Salzmann, a professional himself and one who had played in the orchestra of the Royal Italian Opera Company under Sir Michael Costa, said to himself: 'Here is a professional. I'll treat her as professionals were treated in my day,' and as a consequence most rehearsals ended in chaos, with The Freed sobbing wildly in a corner and Salzmann threatening to throw his hand in and disband the company.

However, we got on somehow. It was all *very* interesting to me. I had rehearsed *Captain Corcoran* in Manchester, and had had to give my part up as I was sailing for Singapore on the day of the first performance, so I had an easy, not to say amusing, time. The opera was being produced by Jules Fabris, who was at that time fairly old and not above an extra *stengah* or two, and as several of the principals were new to the game there was plenty to be amused at.

An innovation was arranged for the performances—which were advertised as being 'on a scale of magnificence new to Singapore'—in the shape of a buffet in the town hall where, as the notice in the paper put it, 'Gentlemen will be able to obtain for their lady friends some lemonade, and for themselves the *stengah* or other suitable beverage.' Singapore had evidently begun to wake up!

Among the people who were making their first appearance on the Singapore stage were Mrs F.W. Barker (Hebe); A.B. Cross

(Sir Joseph Porter); F.G. Keiller (Rackstraw); H.M. Stewart (Deadeye); W.N. Skey (Boatswain). As for me, I was only twenty-three at the time so could be called one of the 'younger set', and then there was The Freed. The only 'old hand' was Mrs Salzmann as Buttercup, so obviously the performances were awaited with great interest.

On 11 September this company of 'youngsters' made its bow to a Singapore audience, and did excellently. The papers praised it extravagantly, calling it the best show—professional or otherwise—seen in Singapore for many a long day. They also remarked that, for the first time in the Farther East, an amateur chorus was 'toeing the footlights' that did not look 'amateur' in the least; rather a big statement to make, I think. But a pinch of salt is really necessary with this remark: 'You could not have found more smartness among Mr George Edwardes' trained angels at the gaiety!' Yes, the papers and the reporters did us well—very well.

However, even allowing for the reporters' enthusiasm, it was a good show, and the big audience was immensely pleased and we were sure of a huge success.

I may mention that when I produced *Pinafore* again about six years ago, I procured from my mother at home a photo of the old performance in 1902, and hung it up on the stage for the company to see. They all roared with laughter at it, and so did I. But comparisons are odious, and the great thing was that we gave Singapore a treat, the like of which they had not had before.

The second performance secured us no less than three columns in *The Straits Times*. I commend this fact to present-day editors, who give local talent a few lines but a column or so to some sordid crime committed on the other side of the world.

Unfortunately I was taken ill on the night of that second performance, and was found hanging out of my window, half unconscious and vomiting blood. No one knew then what was the matter and I was supposed to have burst a blood vessel, but later on we knew that it was the beginning of typhoid—more of that anon, though.

Billy Dunman, always ready to do anything, took my part at a moment's notice, and the show went merrily on—without me. So popular was it that extra performances were given to benefit this and that deserving cause, and I believe it only stopped running because The Freed had to leave Singapore.

I was now out of things; my illness had necessitated a complete rest, and when I was better I took a trip to Penang, of which more anon. While I was away, however, certain events took place which should be recorded in this chronicle as having direct bearing on my own life in Singapore.

The first of these was the decision, come to at a meeting of the Memorial Hall Committee on 27 September, that the conversion of the town hall into a theatre was not only desirable but practical, and Messrs Swan & McLaren were instructed to prepare the necessary plans forthwith. I shall have more to say elsewhere about the actual building of the theatre; it is sufficient here to note the date of its birth.

Another item of interest was the decision, made by a committee which sat to consider Volunteer expenditure, that it was strongly advisable that a permanent adjutant should be appointed from the regular forces. It was this decision that resulted in the bringing out of Captain B.B. Colbeck, the first SO to LF, about whom I have a lot to say in 'The Bad Old Days'!

It will, I think, be interesting to people of the present day to hear how we went to Penang and up the hill thirty years ago. I have before me an account of the first trip I made there in September 1902, and certain passages from my diary give an excellent description of the journey. I propose, therefore, to quote them now in full:

I have just been watching the most glorious sunset I have ever seen. It included two distinct rainbows, and the blending of colours was magnificent. The dark green of the scrub on either side and the light blue–green of the sea all go to make a very lovely picture.

We left Port Swettenham about an hour ago, and are now at the mouth of the northern channel of the Klang River, on our way to Teluk Anson where we should arrive at about half past six tomorrow morning.

Port Swettenham itself is a godforsaken hole, just a clearing in the eternal swamp and jungle with tree stumps still sticking up out of the ground. It is rather an important place though, as it is the terminus of the Selangor State Railway and the port for Kuala Lumpur.

This steamer that I am on, the *Malacca*, is considered to be the crack passenger boat of the Straits Steamship Company's fleet.

She is commanded by Captain Daly, and both he and his ship are great favourites with local travellers, as very good food is obtainable on board and Daly always serves each passenger with a cocktail before dinner at this own expense. The accommodation is, of course, aft and is considerably cleaner than on the other ships for, although no one goes into the cabins below except for the purpose of changing clothes, there do not seem to be as many cockroaches about as one would expect and the cabins are perhaps larger, though, of course, impossibly hot.

Our meals are served on a big skylight with a flat wooden top which runs right down the centre of the first-class deck and at night time, as soon as coffee is over and the tablecloth taken away, the boys bring up the mattresses and place them side by side on the skylight in front of us. It is a literal example of the old sentence, 'Where I eats I sleeps.' But it is a very pleasant bedroom and one gets a comfortable rest, as long as the rain keeps off and the awning is watertight.

I shall have to stop now as it is getting too dark to see to write.

* * *

Today, Wednesday, 1 October, I have made a big day of it. When I went to bed last night the weather gave promise of being fine, but it came on to rain, so that the side awnings had to be put down, and that made things stuffy. I woke at three o'clock in the morning and it was still raining, but I could just make out that

111

we had got into some kind of river. Far away on what should have been the sea side, I could discern a long low-lying point of land. I watched for an hour, and then turned over and went to sleep again. When I awoke again it was half past five and the river had narrowed considerably. The low-lying swampy land was replaced by tall jungle growth, a great deal more luxuriant than that I had seen in the Klang River. I am beginning to see the reason for the statement that the Malay Peninsula has, perhaps, as luxuriant vegetation as any place in the world. The rain had stopped but a white fog hung over everything, not opaque enough to obscure the view but bad enough to give one a very good idea of the deadly dampness of this part of the country.

Soon, we passed a sugar plantation and it did not require the mate's word to assure me that malaria was much more prevalent here than good health. Truly it was a wretched sight to gaze on, and I should think ten times more wretched for the Europeans who had to live there.

I was not at all prepossessed with my first view of Teluk Anson, where we arrived about six o'clock in the morning. Although better than Port Swettenham, there is little else there but the railway terminus. The place has, of course, its club and games ground, but neither looks as if they are much used.

* * *

We—that is, Captain Daly and myself—left for Ipoh by train at about half past eight, and were soon in the middle of the real jungle, through which the railway has been cut. This scenery soon gave way to more open country, however, and we reached the land of the tin-mining industry. The tin here is nearly all alluvial, and all the miners have to do is wash this alluvial sludge and the tin ore is left behind.

Most of the mining is done by Chinese, like all the rest of the work in these parts. A Malay is altogether too lazy, too much of a 'gentleman' to turn his hand to real hard work of this description. He is a farmer by nature and by environment. His padi plot, the fruits of the jungle, the fish he can catch or the game he can snare are enough for him. Even then he lets his womenfolk do most of the field work.

* * *

I do not think much of Ipoh itself. It seems a very dirty place, being full of Chinese miners. No government officials live here; their place is five miles away at a spot called Batu Gajah.

The view, however, from the town is simply superb. The place lies in a valley and all round are the hills, which rise quite suddenly from the plain and are densely wooded the whole way up. Turn which way you will, you can see nothing but the heavily forested hills. As I saw them they looked particularly fine, for dense clouds were rolling round their summits, making the whole effect a very grand sight.

We returned to Teluk Anson by the 2.18 train.

At Teluk Anson, I left the Malacca and boarded the SS *Lady*

Weld, where I am now. She is an old boat with paddle wheels, but seems comfortable, and I have no doubt will be all right as long as the wind keeps down.

It is now so cold that I am wearing my thick European-made Norfolk jacket, and I don't feel too warm in that!

The dinner bell has just rung, so I will stop for tonight.

* * *

Last night, after I finished writing, the rain came down so heavily that the captain could not see a yard in front of him. It was a terrible storm and I have never seen rain like it. We had to anchor for three hours, with anchors out ahead and astern, for we were still in the river and might have run aground if we had tried to go on. A very strong wind was blowing and, in spite of the awning, the rain swept right across the deck from rail to rail. The only light we had was from a few storm lanterns, and altogether it was most eerie, not to say uncomfortable.

However, I got my mattress into some sort of shelter and went to sleep and when I woke, the rain had ceased, it was daylight and we were well in sight of Penang. The entrance from the sea is very pretty, the Penang side being hilly and well wooded with lots of little islands, though the mainland is very flat and uninteresting, and looks very swampy. I understand that the big sugar plantations are here.

* * *

The town of Penang itself lies on the nearest point of land to the mainland, and is quite flat. We arrived about half past eight in the morning and I got a sampan and went on shore, where Goodrich met me. Then I went on to the hotel for some breakfast. I found the hotel small, and a very poor place compared to Raffles Hotel.

After breakfast I had a ride in a rickshaw round the town, called in at Sandilands, Buttery & Co. to see Goodrich again, and went with him to the place where one orders coolies for the ascent of the hill.

At eleven o'clock in the morning I set out on my journey, doing the part to the foot of the hill in a gharry. Arrived at the hill to find the Indian bearers waiting—nine of them—with my 'conveyance'. This consisted of a chair on long poles, which was carried by six men, while my luggage was piled on the heads of the other three.

I got into the chair and we started. It was the most curious kind of locomotion that I have ever experienced, and is possibly very like riding on a camel, though this is only conjecture as I have never ridden on a camel.

Our procession was as follows: First, my big portmanteau carried on one man's head, then the Japanese basket on the head of another, then the third carrying my boy's box with the boy following behind on foot, and lastly, myself in the chair. It must have made a quaint and interesting picture, the dark copper-skinned natives in bright-coloured loincloths and myself in white, wearing a sun helmet and carrying a Japanese umbrella, while all round was the brilliant green of the tropical vegetation.

The ascent is exceedingly steep, hardly ever less than thirty degrees, sometimes up to forty-five degrees and in places to sixty degrees. At times it seemed just as if I was lying back in a long chair, for my feet were often on a level with my chest.

We travelled up a path cut in steps, zigzagging up the mountain side for an hour and a half. On one side the cliffs rose up to a height that made one dizzy, and on the other was a precipice, sometimes sheer, always very steep, for hundreds of feet down. Over all and dominating all was the jungle: real, thick, untouched, great trees rising out of the immensely thick undergrowth, with lesser trees and palms and all kinds of tropical growth. At the lower levels it was intensely hot but, as we ascended, a breeze began to come through the trees which got cooler and fresher as we climbed.

The path is very narrow, having only room for the chair. At times, too, in turning a sharp corner, I and the chair would be slung clear of the corner altogether, and would be literally suspended in mid air over a sheer drop of anything up to one hundred feet and even more. An eerie feeling and, I should think, not very pleasant for those afflicted with nerves.

There is a stillness about the jungle that is different from anything I have ever experienced. It can be best described as a noisy silence for, though there is a constant sound or rustling of leaves, humming of insects, the occasional song of a bird or the chattering of a monkey, there is always that dominating feeling of solitude and loneliness, an absence of human sound which is, to my mind, more silent than the stillest place where mortals are.

With an occasional rest and changes of duty for the coolies, we at length reached the Crag Hotel, my destination, and after settling myself in I spent the rest of the day lying at my window in a long chair and drinking in the beauty of the wonderful view.

*   *   *

This morning we had a lovely walk. There are two planters staying here who have also been ill so, of course, we could not walk very fast or far, but managed to get to the signal station and the governor's house. It was, to be exact, 2,541.37 feet above sea level.

This is the highest inhabited spot on the island, for though Western Hill some miles away is actually higher, there is no habitation there. We stayed for an hour talking to the signal man, who had been home for the coronation with the Volunteer contingent, and then strolled back to the hotel in time for breakfast.

*   *   *

The hotel here is a funny little place. It is built right on the edge of the Crag, and from the dining-room windows—European style, with glass!—there is a sheer drop onto rocks below. Off the dining room are the bedrooms and, at the end of the room opposite the windows, a bar has been erected. There are, of course, no *punkah*s, and the place is lit by oil lamps at night. This evening we have had a wonderful thunderstorm. The lightning has been magnificent, lighting up the whole place and showing us great banks of clouds rolling away below us. We are, of course, well above the clouds but we haven't missed the rain. I have been so cold that I have worn my full suit of Norfolk tweeds, flannel shirt and all, and had to rub my hands together to keep warm.

I felt like doing a five-mile walk but dared not risk it.

* * *

Today I left the hill at ten o'clock in the morning in the chair as before, only this time I went backwards! This is done to prevent one falling out at the steeper parts! It induces a feeling of sickness at times, this travelling the wrong way round. However, all went well and I duly found myself at the bottom of the hill. I paid off my coolies, got a gharry and wended my way to the wharf and the *Lady Weld* where I am now, waiting for the ship to start and finishing off this account of my first real holiday trip in Malaya.

On 22 October the papers published, as a supplement, the proposed plans of the new theatre.

They were slightly different from the plans finally accepted and, funnily enough, did not show the glaring faults that actually occurred when the building was being put up—more of which later.

An interesting little note appeared in the papers at this time headed, 'War office airship, a speed of twenty-five miles an hour.' A Dr Barton seems to have been the inventor, and wood and bamboo were the materials chosen for the venture. Mr F.L. Rawson, the consulting engineer, was enthusiastic—so the paper said—in his belief that, in calm weather, a speed of twenty to twenty-five miles would be obtained, while the engines would be powerful enough to keep the ship stationary against a twenty-mile wind. Wonderful!

To show the level to which the Volunteer Rifles had now descended it is interesting to note that, at a final parade of the SVC in preparation for the King's birthday parade, there were present exactly six members of the SVR! The likeness of the Rifles to Singapore was now a common quip. It was said that, whereas Singapore was a small piece of land entirely surrounded by water, the SVR was a small body of men entirely surrounded by officers!

This year the birthday parade was held for the first time on the racecourse. The presence of a large body of naval men from the ships in port made the numbers on parade too large for the limited accommodation of the padang.

Field officers were all mounted, and I remember that the firing of the *Feu de Joie* caused moments of anxiety to the officers and all ranks of the SVC, the former for fear that they might tumble off, and the latter for fear of the result when the horses stampeded. However, we learnt afterwards that Daddy Abrams, who supplied the mounts, had had them out early with his stable boys and had ridden them to a standstill, so that they would be quiet on parade!

On Thursday, 27 November there appeared in the papers a notice, bordered in heavy black, as follows:

EXCHANGE 1/6–15/16
WITH A WEAK TENDENCY.
KIND FRIENDS ACCEPT THIS,
THE ONLY INTIMATION!

The exchange rate was indeed causing us all grave concern, especially those of us who were paid on a dollar basis. The cost of everything was rising rapidly; goods brought from Europe were getting beyond our means and those on slender salaries were finding it difficult to make ends meet. A commission had been appointed to go into the question of putting the Straits Settlements on a gold basis and eventually, of course, the dollar was fixed at 2sh 4d. But while the slump lasted, we had a very thin time.

On 12 December the 'celebrated' cruiser HMS *Argonaut* arrived in Singapore on her first visit. I use the word celebrated advisedly because she was commanded by Captain George H. Cherry. That statement will convey nothing whatever to the ordinary landsman and perhaps little to the modern seaman, but in those days the name Cherry was a big word in the navy.

Reading one of Bartimeus' books a short while ago, I came across a character in a story that was said to be in possession of the Cherry medal, and a footnote was added to the effect: 'Naval men would know what this meant.' This Captain Cherry was a tartar with a liver! He would refuse to lend the steam pinnace to shore-going men on the grounds that it was a waste of coal, and his poor ship's company had to row themselves in from the man-o'-war anchorage and back if they wanted to come ashore! I once went on the *Argonaut* for dinner in the ward room, and was turned off the ship before coffee because someone at my table had laughed too loudly and disturbed the captain. I was once on the quarterdeck with the officers and saw every one of them disappear down the nearest hole when a bell rang, leaving me standing alone in my glory to receive a sentry with the message, 'Captain's compliments, sir, and there's *too much noise*!'

Captain Cherry had the best lot of fellows as officers that I have ever had the pleasure of meeting—only the very best could stick it. The men who had served with him finally clubbed together and struck a medal, which was duly presented to anyone who had survived three years under the redoubtable captain!

Hence the 'Cherry medal'.

My particular pal on board was the then Torpedo-Lieutenant A.H.C. Candy, who had been on the Submarine A1 when she sank in Portsmouth Harbour (I think it was), and only he and the boatswain were saved.

I saw a lot of Candy in Singapore and afterwards in Japan, but more of that anon.

On 16 December the Rev. H.C. Dunkerley was instituted and inducted Archdeacon of Singapore.

I was not present at the time, having then left for Bangkok, but I mention that matter now as it has a bearing upon an incident which will be recounted in due course.

I had been keeping very quiet since my illness in September, and had not taken part in any of the sports or social activities that had gone on.

Early in December my firm decided that they would like a first-hand report about Bangkok trade, which was now assuming great importance in Singapore. I was deputed to make the trip.

An account of that very interesting visit to Bangkok must be left for another chapter.

7

December 1902

I sailed for Bangkok on 5 December 1902 on the SS *Deli*, belonging to the North German Lloyd local service, and the only European passenger boat on the run. With the exception of Chinese-owned steamers, the sea trade to Bangkok was wholly in the hands of the Germans, who some few years before had bought up an English line that was in a bad way and so cornered the business.

On the boat with me was H.W. Noon of Arthur Barker & Co. and Messrs Frizell and Nicholson, managers respectively of the Chartered and Hong Kong Banks. There had been trouble with the Siamese Government over exchange, and the two were going up in a great hurry to a conference to see if they couldn't induce a more reasonable attitude on the part of the government. I believe they succeeded in their mission.

We left Singapore at five o'clock on a Friday evening, and by eight o'clock had passed the Horsburgh Lighthouse and were well on our way round the most southerly point of the Malay Peninsula.

A glance at a map of these parts will show that Bangkok itself is west of Singapore, as far as longitude is concerned, and as the north-east monsoon was blowing strongly, our course was set right across the Gulf to get under lee of the Cochin–China shore. We were fortunate in missing really rough weather—for it can be very bad here—and when we reached the coast, turned and ran along it, going at times almost due west. It was funny to watch the sun set right over the bows of the ship. It made one feel that one was sailing for home.

Funnily enough, on this little steamer, 9,000 miles away from home, there were three Manchester men among the passengers: Noon, myself and a Mr Blass, travelling for Jaffe & Sons!

On the Sunday we saw a curious sight. We passed through mile after mile of fish spawn. It lay on the top of the sea and stretched away to the horizon on either side. A dirty yellow in colour, it looked just as if one had taken a painter's brush and daubed the top of the sea with distemper. Darting in and out among it were hundreds of sea snakes, generally about a yard long, of a bright yellow colour and with brilliant green spots on their backs. Flying fish were also abundant here. The Gulf of Siam is, of course, a very lonely spot, ships being few and far between, and it must be simply teeming with fish and all kinds of marine life.

We reached the coast of Siam about one o'clock on the Monday, and during the afternoon were running up it fairly close inshore. It looked very wild; there did not seem to be any sign of human habitation though I believe it was, at that time, sparsely populated. The cliffs were very steep and generally the coast reminded me of the approach to Aden from the Indian Ocean. The leaden-coloured hills, rising one above the other like gigantic sand dunes, were a very fair imitation of the Arabian coast, and altogether the view was not very inspiring.

Later on, however, the aspect of the coast changed. Green began to show itself and soon the hills seemed to be covered with what, from the sea, looked like heather or gorse. Islands, generally of small dimensions, were numerous, but on none of them, or on the mainland, could be noticed any sign of forest such as one gets in Malaya.

We ran through these islands before the sun set, and then seemed to lose sight of land for a time. At about eight o'clock in the evening we sighted the flashlight at the mouth, or rather one of the mouths, of the Chao Phraya River, on which Bangkok is situated. We dropped anchor at ten o'clock as we had to wait for the tide to cross the bar, and did not move off up the river till eight o'clock the next morning.

Soon after we anchored at the bar, a Siamese gunboat came alongside and a very good-looking, young naval officer in a white uniform plastered with gold lace stepped on board our ship. What surprised me the most was that he was wearing spurs!

He had come on board to greet a Siamese prince who was returning to his country after having spent six years at Eton.

Going up the river it was quite cold, and it was necessary to walk briskly about the deck to keep warm.

I have before me as I write the diary of that trip to Bangkok, and as it was faithfully kept day by day and gives a very good account of our doings and the interesting sights we saw, I cannot do better than quote it as it stands.

Here goes, therefore:

We crossed the bar yesterday morning at eight o'clock, and were soon steaming up Chao Phraya River. In no place is it wide; even at the mouth I should say that it is not more than a mile and a half at most, and it narrows rapidly until the breadth is not more than two or three hundred yards. Be that as it may, you can travel up it in a native boat for six weeks! Just about the time it would take you to get home and back again. Think of it for a minute, and try and imagine it.

The banks of the river are low and swampy. In fact they are very much like those of the Klang River in the Native States. They differ from the latter, however, in the fact that they seem to be thickly populated. Indeed, villages seem to spring up every few hundred yards. The houses are all built on piles in the river, and the 'streets' are raised causeways, so that the general effect is very picturesque. Temples, too, are scattered over the land and seem to be built in all shapes and sizes. One I noticed particularly for it was an exact reproduction of a native junk, done in white and red stone. Instead of masts it had three tapering steeples. A lot of these so-called temples are, however, only graves. I believe it depends greatly on the position of the deceased in native society whether his tomb is large or small, and what shape it takes. Of course, the prevailing religion is Buddhism, but here and there can be seen Chinese settlements containing their own little temples. One does not seem to be able to get away from the Chinese, except by going right away home to England. Europe seems to be the only continent they haven't yet reached.

There are several forts dotted along the banks, all of them flying the tremendous red flag with the white elephant on it, which is the emblem of the Siamese nation, and also the flag of its royal house.

We arrived at Bangkok proper about eleven o'clock and, after waiting some time, Noon and I got a lift with our luggage in the post office launch and were dropped at the hotel steps soon after. The river here is the great highway. Everyone owns launches; all the big business houses are on the river and one can go for miles and miles and never get outside of the town. As I sit now, overlooking the river, I can see the little launches puffing up and down and making a tremendous noise, until I can almost imagine I am back in Hamburg docks again!

The Oriental Hotel, where Noon and I now find ourselves, is the best in the town, but it is a most filthy hole and very badly managed. The food is simply inedible, besides being very dirtily served up. Still, there is no other and so we must make the best of it and try and get some decent food at the United Club, to which we have been elected as visiting members.

After we had had tiffin and seen our rooms, Noon went off in a launch to see some friends while I strolled into the Chartered Bank next door, thinking I would change my money. But to my surprise they wouldn't change Singapore dollars at all, and so I can't get any money! You may have read about the currency question in the papers. The Siamese Government have suddenly decided to use gold, and have fixed an exchange rate which

127

doesn't suit the banks so they won't do any business. I am landed in an out-of-the-way country with four hundred dollars which, here, are not worth the trouble of tearing up! A nice predicament, isn't it? However, I have still got a lead pencil and can sign my name, and if they want money they'll have to take my dollars or do without.

Noon came along to the hotel soon after this, and we then went to the Bangkok United Club to meet some men who had promised to put us up for membership. We had dinner there and, I am sorry to say, stayed there very late afterwards as we were introduced to such a lot of men that we couldn't possibly get away. We decided always to have tiffin and dinner at the club as it was so much nicer than the hotel, and this rule we have rigidly adhered to. In fact, the hotel food is so bad and is served up so filthily that it is very probable we should be ill if we ate it. It is so hot here just now that one has to be very careful about the food eaten.

We left the club about eleven o'clock in the evening, and went to see a Malay theatre play. It was very funny but got very tiring, and we soon left. It is curious that, although this same native theatrical company has been in Singapore dozens of times, I had never seen a Malay show at all until I came to Siam. Only when one gets out of a place does one learn a great deal more about it than when living in it!

After leaving the theatre, on our way home, we went into a gambling saloon—a wonderfully big place where all the gambling is done on the floor. The game was *fantan*, a Chinese gambling game which is played all over the East. It is the same game that is played at Johore near Singapore. The size of the floor space played on and the dexterity of the croupiers, of whom there are four, is the most interesting part. The Siamese women are the most inveterate gamblers and outnumber the men in such places as these by five to one!

Leaving this place, we considered it about time to go home to bed. We got to the hotel about half past twelve, which was not bad considering everything.

11 December 1902

Yesterday we had a most interesting time visiting all round. I set off about half past nine in the morning to have a look round the place and see if I could find any of my Singapore Chinamen's friends. The worst part about it was that the men in Singapore always have their own Chinese names for the different streets, and it was therefore of no use asking for their addresses in Bangkok as they simply didn't know them. However, I had one man's address and I therefore set off to find him, intending to press him into my service when found, and to make him show me around.

I therefore hired a gharry—a sort of two-pony open carriage, driven by a little Siamese boy—and set off. My way lay right along the main road, which ran for miles parallel to the river. Finally we turned down a street and stopped at the door of my man's shop. He was a very affable chap, and was very glad to show me round. I spent the morning delivering my letters of introduction, and generally looking round.

After knocking about in the terrible heat for about three hours I began to feel rather tired. As it was nearly one o'clock, I drove back to the club where Noon and I had arranged to have tiffin.

There we met a man called Mr O'Shea, the chief electrician of the Tramways and Electric Lighting Company. He was very jolly and offered, if we had nothing to do, to show us round in the afternoon. As he has been in the country nearly fifteen years and knows everybody and everything connected with the place, you may be sure that we accepted his offer with alacrity.

After tiffin, therefore, we started in two carriages and drove along the chief road for about three miles until we came to the Electric Lighting Station. O'Shea showed us all over this, and I must say that I was exceedingly surprised to see the whole plant on such modern lines. But everything seems to be done by electricity here. The trams are driven by it, the whole town and all the houses (even down to little native shops) are lit by it, while all the clubs, palaces and private houses contain electric fans! Electric light has been penetrated into the Buddhist temples and now, by an ingenious arrangement of footlights, buddha is beautifully lit up of an evening!

After leaving the station, O'Shea said he was going to take us to a bazaar, or at least what would be a bazaar in two days. But what a bazaar! It was, like most bazaars, in aid of the church, being ostensibly to provide enough marble to cover a new temple; but in other respects it was entirely different. Fancy King Edward, with all the royal family to help him, standing in an ordinary booth and raffling his own portrait! And yet this is what the King of Siam does at these shows, which are held once a year.

The bazaar is held in Dusit Park, a kind of country residence recently built and laid out by the King.

Our way there lay through beautifully wide roads, bordered with young trees. According to O'Shea, the area was impassable swamp not very many years ago. However, one day the King expressed a wish to have a palace on this particular spot, so a palace had to be built.

We got to the place where the bazaar was to be held but, instead of a wonderful confusion of stalls already in their keepers' hands, as we expected, we could see nothing but an enormous array of bare poles. On expressing our view that the thing didn't look like much, O'Shea told us to wait until the next night and see the difference!

The Siamese, it appears, are the most casual people on the face of this earth, and are always leaving things until the very last possible minute, but in cases like this they are never late. Here was this tremendous place, half a mile square, hardly pegged out for the stalls. Yet they were going to get it ready, and expected O'Shea to put something like 35,000 electric lamps up, in a day and a night. And they did it! But how do you think? Why, the King simply sent an order to the whole of the navy to go and put the thing up! There's a potentate for you! When we were there the navy were swarming all over the place like bees, and even princes of the royal house were knocking in nails and hauling planks about. Such is the power wielded by an Eastern monarch.

Leaving this place we drove to the palace of the King and,

owing to the fact that O'Shea is such a well-known man, were admitted. By the way, O'Shea is the only European who has been admitted to the royal harem. He went there to put up the electric light!

The palace is a most imposing place, surrounded by a tremendously strong wall, like the Tower of London. It is formed of three squares, one inside the other. The innermost contains the private apartments of the King and one is not allowed inside there, unless on a special occasion. Next to this is the square containing the temples etc. while outside this again are the government buildings, War Office, Foreign Office, etc.

The buildings in the outermost square are very fine, but are quite on the European plan and look very much like our own government offices in London. Inside the second wall, however, one drops right into the centre of the Buddhist religion, so to speak, and it is a very curious change.

We knocked at the door of the big temple, and after a time were admitted by a shrivelled-up old man in a yellow toga, a real Buddhist priest. Through this gate we came to a place which looked very like an English cathedral's cloisters, the walls of which were covered with the most beautiful allegorical paintings. We looked at these and at the curious and, in many cases, hideous figures which were scattered about, and then went through another door and up the steps to the temple proper. And, oh! What a sight it was! Try and imagine a building somewhere about the size of a cathedral nave, only square, covered with most marvellous moulding all worked in gold leaf, and picked out with myriads of little pieces of cut glass of all colours of the rainbow. Try and imagine a tremendous dome, one mass of polished gold and, again, a pair of huge doors standing fully twenty feet high, wholly inlaid with silver and mother-of-pearl. Imagine again the whole of this wonderful mass glinting and scintillating in the rays of an Eastern sun, and you get a very poor idea of the effect produced on us, as we stood there, wondering, awestruck, at the glorious spectacle.

But when the doors swung open and we entered at the bidding of the priest who stood there, and closed the door behind us, the change from the brilliant sun to the semi-darkness of the interior blinded us for a moment. But when we could use our eyes it needed no one to tell us that we were standing amid a mass of untold wealth. In the half light we could see tier upon tier of great gold ornaments, extending upwards for forty feet and terminating in something that looked very like the eye of a cat, green in the dark. It seemed to wink at us as we looked.

The priest threw open a window and we saw, perched on the top of that forty-feet pile of gold, a little image of a buddha, standing about two feet high and of a curiously dull green colour in the daylight. That buddha is absolutely the most expensive image of the god in the world, so we were told, being cut out of a solid mass of jade stone. And the diamonds in the place! And the rubies, sapphires and emeralds in untold numbers! I broke the Tenth Commandment about 120 times a minute, I think, for I could not help wanting to have my hands in some of the piles of precious stones that were heaped together in places, as if the priests were tired of trying to find room for them on the altar and had swept them up as one would sweep crumbs. And yet what a revulsion of feeling one gets, while walking round, to come upon a cheap German clock in the midst of all this barbaric splendour. At first it is a shock, but after a time one gets used to seeing a diamond star, worth at least £25,000, lying calmly alongside a flower vase made in Germany. The average native really has no sense of the value of things, and in the different temples one meets all sorts of curious mixtures such as I have mentioned. But it must be remembered that all these valuables and worthless articles have been sent to the temple as presents for the god, and therefore are entitled to the same amount of care and respect.

We got out of the temple somehow without taking anything; the priest as we left giving us a handful of scented flowers, and we in return presenting him with a piece of money.

Then O'Shea took us for a drive round, or rather along the town, for Bangkok is built on either bank of the Chao Phraya River and although the town is, I should think, fully six miles long, in no place is it more than one mile broad, and often dwindles down to a few hundred yards. We passed the barracks where the funny little soldiers were drilling, looking very like a box of leaden men. We stopped for a little while to listen to their band practising in the barrack square. They don't play so badly and keep very good time, but as their brass instruments are all differently tuned, the effect given to 'Annie Laurie', which they were playing, was somewhat painful.

Driving on we passed a squadron of their cavalry, mounted

on little ponies born and bred in Siam, none more than eleven to twelve hands high. They looked very funny indeed, for the men, as small in proportion as the ponies themselves, wore great top boots with big spurs and had wonderful swords, almost as big as themselves, dangling at their sides, with the old-fashioned sabretache of Crimean War days.

We got back to the club about five o'clock in the afternoon. Then we went on to the hotel, changed and set off calling, but only managed to call upon the American ambassador, as it was too late to do more. We again dined at the club and finished up the evening playing billiards and generally amusing ourselves.

12 December 1902

Yesterday we did nothing much in the way of sightseeing. We both set off early in the morning on our business, and did not meet until tiffin time. My work took me across the river, which I navigated in a Siamese sampan. These are rather curious boats and I should think particularly hard to row, for the men only use one oar. Instead of using another oar, they balance the boat by standing on the bulwark and leaning over slightly. You will probably understand what I mean if you look at a picture of a Venetian gondola.

The day again was frightfully hot and the sun was terrible. Usually at this time of the year in Siam people are wearing woollen clothing but owing, as it is said, to the eruptions taking place all over the world and the curious climatic conditions experienced, the cold weather has failed to come this year, and it is as hot as

135

ever. I got frightfully tired and hot with walking about, and after tiffin was fit for nothing at all. Noon was in the same condition, and so we both had a snooze. At four o'clock we set out to pay some more calls, and called upon Mrs Forbes of the Chartered Bank and Mrs Skinner, both of whom Noon had known at one time in Singapore.

That evening we made arrangements with a friend to have a big day on Sunday. We are to go to Ayuthia, or some such name, the ancient capital of the country about seventy miles inland. I hope it will be a good day.

We are getting to bed later and later! Last night it was half-past one before we turned in. If this goes on much longer I shall want every hour of the four and a half days at home to make up for lost time in sleep.

13 December 1902

Yesterday was very much like the day before, still frightfully hot and very hard to work in.

Since I arrived here I have been very much puzzled to tell the difference between the men and women. With the lower classes it is exceedingly difficult as they both wear exactly the same clothes put on in the same way; and to make it more confusing, the women do the same work, and work as hard, as the men. I crossed the river again today and couldn't for the life of me tell if it was a man or woman who rowed me across.

There are a tremendous lot of Chinese in the place and, as far as I can see, they do all the business just as they do in every Eastern town they are allowed to go to. Some day they will overrun the whole world, for there is no doubt that they are the finest race of businessmen living.

There are a tremendous quantity of uniformed men in the streets too. I counted five different kinds of policemen all of different races! Even the tram guard wears a wonderful uniform of khaki and red. The soldiers mostly wear blue trousers and grey coat like the Russians, and do not look at all smart. The navy, as usual, look the smartest in their white and blue and, as in England, they are the handy men of the country and can do anything from putting up electric lighting to building a palace. The only thing, unfortunately, that they no good at is sailoring, which is a pity!

Yesterday afternoon we paid some more calls, and afterwards went out to dinner at the residence of Mr Brockmann, the head of Windsor & Co. and a friend of Mr Sergels. We got away from there at half-past one, and didn't get to bed until two o'clock in the morning. We are getting on!

Saturday

Today, or rather this afternoon and evening, has been a great day. I did my business as usual, and had tiffin at the club. Our tiffin was notable from the fact that we had it with Prince Sittapon, a grandson of the King. He is an awfully jolly little chap, about nineteen years old, and has been educated at Harrow. He was introduced to us by our friend, O'Shea, who is very friendly with all these royal folk.

In the afternoon, Noon and I went out to a lady and

gentleman's house to have a game of tennis, which did us a lot of good. There we met our friend, Mr Jack, who has promised to take us to the ancient capital tomorrow. He says he will call for us at half past six tomorrow morning, but as we are certain not to be in bed tonight until two tomorrow morning (Irish), I'm afraid we may be a minute or two late. However, I have told my boy to call us both at a quarter to six, and as he isn't keeping late nights, no doubt he'll be able to do so. We are now going out to dinner with a Mr and Mrs Skinner, and are then all going on to the Royal Dusit Park Fair.

Later

Dinner with Mrs Skinner was very enjoyable. A Mr and Mrs Roberts were there; we are to dine with them on Wednesday.

After dinner we didn't sit long, but all set off at about nine o'clock in gharries and traps for this wonderful fair. We had a very pleasant three-mile drive. Noon and I arrived first for Noon sat back in the carriage with the whip and tickled the ponies from behind, while I encouraged the driver. Didn't we fly along! I've never been for such a fast drive in my life. It was fairly dangerous, too, for we turned corners at full speed and never on more than two wheels out of the four. However, the Siamese have evidently learnt the ways of the curious Englishman, and they stepped to one side with nothing more than a guttural 'Ma'. It is so easy to say and means such a lot that it is a favourite expression.

Arriving at the fair we were really bewildered! Could this be the place that two days ago was simply a wilderness? Lit up with myriads of fairy electric lights, gay with flags and bunting of all colours of the rainbow, the stalls simply laden over with the most costly goods of Siam, it would have been something to talk about in England if it had been put up there in a month. Yet these lazy-looking, easy-going Siamese had managed it, including the putting up of 35,000 electric lamps, in a day and a half. Truly the Oriental can work if he likes.

We made our way first to the billiard saloon where a tournament was being held. A Siamese prince had presented a gold cup to be competed for by the sixteen best players in Bangkok, eight Europeans and eight Siamese. The Europeans were all knocked out in the second round, and the Siamese had it amongst themselves. I sat with Mrs Roberts for some time watching Mr Roberts play, and then we got bored and went for a walk round. But we hadn't got very far when a grand-looking official stopped us and turned us back, saying the King was at dinner. We tried another way, but that evidently led past the back of his chair for they wouldn't let us go that way either. Finally coming to a small river, we crossed one of the numerous bridges, intending to recross some distance down. When we had gone far enough we turned to go over a bridge. But a man like a lictor, carrying a bundle of rods, said we couldn't go that way as it led to the part of the show set aside for the King's harem. I said some very rude things to that poor man, and asked him if the bundle of canes he was carrying was to whack the little girls with when they were naughty; but he didn't answer as, of course, he couldn't understand English, which is perhaps just as well.

You may not believe me, but the only bridge (and there were many) by which we were allowed to cross that wretched stream was the one we had come over by. Turning down a passage that led to the so-called American Bar where we thought we might get something to sustain us, we were stopped by a very little man with a very big sword who said we couldn't go that way as the King was having a drink! All my explanations that we were practically, and to all intents and purposes, a king and queen ourselves as we, too, wanted a drink (in fact had wanted one for some time), were to no avail, and back we had to go.

We spent some time systematically breaking the Tenth Commandment, looking at all the beautiful silver, gold and clay Siamese ware displayed, and regularly asking the prices of all the things we knew were too expensive to buy, just to relieve our feelings a little. We happened to be in one stall looking at a magnificent book bound in embossed silver when, hearing a noise behind me, I turned round and there I saw those wretched officials clearing the way for the King, who was going round the stalls. I told Mrs Roberts and suggested we should be going because, for all I knew, we might be in the King's stall. If anyone is caught there by him they generally leave it the poorer by about 2,000 ticals (baht). However, Mrs Roberts said it wasn't the King's stall and there she was and there she was going to stop, king or no king. So we remained where we were.

Presently he came along followed by about thirty gentlemen of the household, and entered the very stall we were standing in, so that I got a good look at him. He is a little chap, about five foot two or three inches, not more. He has a fairly ugly face with a drooping moustache, but his appearance is greatly improved by the expression on his face, which is a very kindly one. He bought the book I mentioned and then left, raising his hat and bowing politely to Mrs Roberts as he departed. One curious thing about him that I noticed was that, in spite of his exalted rank, he chews that disgusting betel nut. While he was in the stall he beckoned to one of the suites, who immediately came forward with a big gold bowl—the royal spittoon—got down on one knee and held the bowl up for the King to use! It is a beastly habit when carried to excess, and disfigures the lips horribly.

After the King had passed, we strolled on round the show and held conversations with various princesses who held stalls, which I must say made me very bashful as the costume of the ladies in question was, to say the least of it, very rational. However, I got used to it in time, and even went so far as to purchase one or two things from one of the stalls where, as a consequence, I was horribly 'done' in the matter of price.

We then wended our way to a big Siamese theatre, which was under the management of one of the head princesses. We didn't stay long, however, only just long enough to get an idea of what the show was like. The stage comes a way out to the front, and is very like a big marquee with the sides taken away. You might imagine it best as an enormous dining-room oblong table. At one of the short ends is the scenery, and round the other three sides the audience sit.

The play we were watching was very gorgeous, as far as

costumes went, but was not of much interest to us as there was very little talking, most of the time being taken up by native dancing which isn't dancing at all, but consists of moving the limbs and body in all sorts of curious ways. One thing that interested me much was the way the lady dancers worked their hands. You've probably seen pictures of the Burmese dancers with their fingers bent back almost touching their wrists. They do this seemingly without any effort whatsoever, but it is not a pretty sight in my opinion, and cannot by the widest stretch of imagination be called graceful.

After half an hour of this we had had about enough, and went out just in time for a great procession of Buddhist priests. All the priests in Bangkok were supposed to take part and there were, I believe, close to a thousand of them. It was a most curious and weird sight to see all these men, some fully ninety years old, every one of them dressed in the yellow toga of the priesthood and all carrying a lit stick of incense. The smell, of course, was something abominable, but we didn't mind it in time, although I can hardly say we got used to it.

During the evening I had a very funny experience with the parson of HMS *Albion*, which happened to be in Bangkok at the time. He wished to go into the big temple in the centre of the fair where the seven-ton brass buddha, in whose honour and for whose benefit the fair was, was situated. I had been in two or three times before, and he would have me go in again with him. We were walking boldly up the temple steps when I suddenly discovered the place was somehow different from when I had been in it last. I soon found that this was accounted for by the fact that the whole of the altar and the approaches to it were lit up with little sticks of incense, burning brightly and giving a sort of Christmas tree look to the whole show.

We walked slowly forward, through rows of Buddhists with their heads on the ground, praying, when suddenly we were tapped on the shoulder. Turning round we beheld an old priest with his arms full of incense tapers and holy flowers which he proceeded to shove into the padre's hands. He then gave him a box of matches and, with a low bow, intimated by his gestures that the parson should at once proceed and burn incense before the buddha. He kept pushing us forward until we were right at the altar steps, and the parson's face was a study! I could hardly keep from laughing, it was so funny. It was plain to see that the parson was in a horrible funk, for he didn't want to burn incense and he didn't quite know what would happen to him if he didn't. I'm sure he thought he was going to be killed there and then.

I didn't enlighten him upon the fact that this was only the native way of showing politeness, and that he could very easily give the sticks back to the priest. Standing there with his arms full of flowers and joss sticks at the foot of buddha, and gazing wildly round for some loophole of escape, he looked too funny for anything.

Suddenly he spied a side door down a passage and, dropping all his sticks and things, he grabbed me frantically by the arm and bolted. He got out safely and, I believe, thinks to this day that his promptness in seeing that door saved both his life and mine. How

Noon and I did laugh when I told him about it afterwards.

Sunday

Sunday—at least I think it was Sunday but I'm not sure—was the occasion of a great treat for us. We had been invited by a friend to go a picnic with him to the old capital of Siam, now nothing but a few ruins in the jungle about fifty miles from Bangkok on the river. The name of the place is Ayuthia—at least it sounds like that.

But let me begin at the beginning. The night before, or rather that same morning, Noon and I had got to bed somewhere between half past two and three (Bangkok is a fearful place), and we were awakened at seven by our friend, Jack, to catch an eight o'clock train on the only railway in Siam. It runs for about sixty miles along the river and that is all. Well, we got our tickets and took our seats, or rather all the seats in the carriage for we had plenty of food and drink with us to beguile the tedious hours in the train. Oh, I forgot to tell you that we had Mr Blass, the man from Manchester, with us.

The journey by rail is the most tedious one I've ever experienced. Try and fancy yourself travelling over a country of one uniform colour, a vivid green, with nothing in the world to break it except here and there one of the great dikes, or *klong*s as they are called, intersecting the landscape. Try and imagine that country *all* below sea level, stretching to the horizon all round, and then call to your memory the fact that the horizon doesn't end it, but that it goes on and on like that, with no break whatever, for over four hundred miles. You then get an idea of a dreary landscape. And oh, the unutterable dreariness of the Siamese padi or rice fields. The railway is, of course, built on a causeway and all around is green swamp, swamp, swamp, everything swamp. Huts of mud built on swamp, buffaloes covering themselves with thick layers of swamp to keep the mosquitoes off, and looking ever so much like a lump of the swamp itself. Scantily clad natives up to their waists in it and looking as if they were never made to be anywhere else, their very colour being that of the swamp they belong to. Oh, it is awful, and I can tell you we were quite depressed when we arrived at our journey's end, Railway Head, and got out of the train onto the banks of the river.

But we soon recovered our spirits again, for it was a lovely day, and the river banks, being covered with a certain amount of scrub and jungle, made everything look nice again. They gave a fitting background to the curious little floating village that had 'drifted' (one can hardly say 'sprung up') about the station on the side of the river. These floating villages are most curious. They are not built on piles but actually float on the river, and one gets the impression that a strong wind would break them all up, and send the houses floating down the river, until they happened to drift into another backwater and stop. One can imagine the occupants waking up in the morning and finding that not only they but their house as well had 'flitted' and gone to live in some other town!

Every house has its boat rowed, as I have said already, by one oar only. To beguile the time, and also for a lark, I took Blass for a row in one. I borrowed the boat when the owner wasn't looking, but all I could do was to take it round and round in a circle. It seemed to me that the easiest thing to do with those boats was to upset them. I just managed to miss doing this, however, and as the boat came round to land again in one of its numerous circles, we got out. Blass was rude enough to say he'd had quite enough of that, and as I couldn't induce either Noon or Jack to come for a shilling sail round the bay à la Morecambe I had to get out too.

Jack had a launch waiting for us, and he, Noon and I got in, Blass going back to Bangkok again by train.

We steamed farther up the river by the launch for about fifteen minutes, and then came to our journey's end. This was the house of the only white men in the place. If I remember rightly one of them was called Patteson. He and his father lived here and carried on a business of timber merchants, cutting down the valuable trees in the forest that had grown up round the ancient city and sending them in rafts down to Bangkok for sale. At intervals along the river which, as I have told you, runs inland and is navigable for a six-week journey, you find such men as these, living a very lonely life and sometimes, in the case of those farther up the river, never seeing another of their kind from one year's end to the other. You can imagine, then, how welcome a white man, even a stranger, is, and certainly Patteson was awfully pleased to see us.

As Jack had told him before that we were coming, he had a big tiffin prepared for us. By the time we had had a wash and brush up we were quite ready for it, and the four of us (Patteson's father was away) had an awfully jolly meal.

After tiffin we had a lie down and a smoke for digestion's

sake, and then set off about three o'clock in the afternoon to have a look at the ruins of the old city.

The actual city itself stood about three miles away from where we were, right in the jungle on the other side of the river; but just opposite Patteson's house there were plenty of ruins to give us an idea of them.

We crossed over the river, therefore, and first paid our respects to the governor of the district, whose house was nearby. He was a most affable gentleman, very polite, and seemed very pleased to see us. He is a bit of an antiquarian in his own little Eastern way, and had got together a very fine museum of relics which he had picked up during his years of office, and had very carefully labelled them all. It was exceedingly interesting to notice the different idols which he had collected. The oldest, dated goodness knows how many years ago, seemed to me to be more like the Chinese images than anything else, and I believe it is a fact that the Mongolians overran Siam, the same as they did China, many, many years ago. Then, of later date, Indian and Burman gods could be seen and, of course, these mostly consisted of buddhas of various shapes and forms, although I noticed many of the Hindu gods in the collection.

One thing that interested me immensely was the carving. Of course, both Siamese and Burmese are exceedingly clever at carving, and the metal work of gold and silver was also very fine.

After having examined the curiosities to our hearts' content, we went in the direction of an old tower standing 150 feet high which, we were told, was part of the old royal residence. In fact it was the only part now standing. By dint of careful going we eventually managed to get to the top, and from there got a most magnificent view of the surrounding country and all the ruins. We could see the place where the annual elephant hunt takes place.

The air was so nice and the view so fine that we stayed up the tower for nearly an hour. All the various landmarks of the surrounding country were pointed out to us. When we came down again it was quite time for tea, so, after thanking our kind host for his hospitality in showing us round, we went back with Patteson across the river to his bungalow and had another good feed.

After this was over it was time for us to start for home. We had arranged to go back to Bangkok by the river and to enable us to do this, Jack had sent a launch up the river overnight, laden with provisions etc. It was waiting for us when we got to Patteson's place.

After saying our goodbyes and thanking Patteson for the good time he had given us, we boarded the launch and started. It was by that time just beginning to get dark, and was delightfully cool and nice. We set to work to make ourselves as comfortable as circumstances would permit, as we had a six-hour journey before us and might possibly want to go to sleep for a while.

For some time our way led us through high banks, well wooded as far as the Siamese trees would allow it to be. There were no big trees—more undergrowth than anything else—but it was thick enough. Then the country got to the flat, uninteresting padi (or rice) fields again, and as it was now about eight o'clock and quite dark, we decided that a supper would be advisable. I myself could hardly eat anything. I was feeling very ill indeed just then and could only lie down; every time I tried to sit up a terrible feeling of nausea came over me. Of course, now I know it was the beginnings of typhoid, but at the time I couldn't understand it at all.

Presently the country became more wooded and the banks much steeper, and just about then the moon rose. Even I, ill as I felt, could not but be impressed by the beauty of the scene. There we were, in that little launch, absolutely alone in an unknown country, to us at all events, and not altogether away from danger as the river was very full of rocks and the channel tortuous.

Now we were coming to the most exciting part of the journey. A little way ahead of us the river split into two, one stream going about five miles round an island, meeting the other stream about a mile below the split. This longer channel was, of course, the safe one, as the river runs fairly slowly. The shorter channel was full of rocks and rapids for its length of one mile. It was dangerous, too dangerous for ordinary traffic even in daylight; so I suppose that was why we three Englishmen decided to take the launch that way by moonlight. Such is the contrariness of human nature.

I, in spite of my sickness, could not help but be affected by the excitement and, as we were nearing the junction, lent a hand with the others in putting everything movable in a safe place. Presently we came to the spot where the regular channel turned sharply away to the left. In front of us was the low, thickly wooded island splitting up the river, and away on our right were the rapids. Soon came the cry, 'Hold on all,' and away we went into the roaring waters, our speed almost doubling itself every minute. The little launch rocked and groaned under us; we could not make ourselves heard above the noise of the seething waters. All we could do was to sit tight, hold on and gather what confidence we could from the calm, impassive face of the Siamese at the wheel. With the accustomed stolidity of his race, he looked as if he had spent his life in a launch in shooting rapids at ten o'clock at night.

What a curious revulsion of feeling came over me as, turning my eyes away from that mass of roaring, seething waters, I looked up at the beautiful shining moon. It was riding there calmly in the heavens and perhaps, who knows? wondering what mad thing Englishmen would do next. Even the noise of the waters seemed to fade away as one looked up.

Well, we were through it at last after having many narrow squeaks from rocks that seemed to rise up out of the water as we whirled past, as if vainly trying to stay our mad career. Although I have not actually tried it, I can imagine it would be no joke to run nose onto one of those rocks at the speed of about twenty miles an hour.

We soon began to come into inhabited regions again, passed rice mills, villages and other launches puffing about. Now and again, too, we would pass those great rafts of valuable timber, mostly teak, floating down the river on the tide, sometimes as much as 300 or 400 yards long. Many of them had probably been coming down the river for months, some perhaps years, and quite respectable villages had grown up on them. They are sent down from the great virgin forests at the head of this most wonderful river. The selection of the trees is made by white men from firms like the Borneo Company and Bombay Burmah Company, Arracan Company, etc., who eat, sleep, and have their being in the unexplored regions away in the north, probably never seeing another of their kind from one year's end to the other.

At midnight we were steaming through the man-o'-war anchorage, off the royal palace, and had a good moonlight view of that wonderful fleet. The sailors of these fleets can do almost anything but sail and the ships, which in nearly all cases but that of the royal yacht, have never left the river since they first came in over the bar. The bar of the river is worth more to Siam than all its naval strength put together.

At half past twelve we pulled up at the steps of the hotel and, after thanking Jack for the marvellously good and enjoyable day he had given us, we turned in. As you may guess, we were content to tumble in behind the mosquito curtains and sleep the sleep of the thoroughly tired.

We spent one delightful evening at Mrs Roberts', Noon and I taking our songs. Both Mrs Skinner and Mrs Roberts are exceedingly fond of music, the former being really a fine pianist. We therefore had good fun.

There is one item of interest to Noon and myself, however, that I might mention here, in the light of what happened afterwards. The day before we returned to Singapore, Noon and I were engaged to spend the afternoon with a Mr and Mrs Phillips, the headmaster of the King's college. Curiously enough, I had once met them both on one of my jaunts to the Native States, and we had met and renewed our acquaintance at a dance held at the Bangkok Club in honour of the *Albion*, the then flagship of the China Squadron.

Well, we made our way to the King's college and spent a very enjoyable afternoon, getting in some good tennis against Phillips and the second master, a Cambridge man the same as Phillips was, and an old rugby player (I'm not sure if the hadn't got his 'blue').

The sequel to the incident occurred about two months later, while I was so ill in hospital. One Sunday evening our chaplain, Mr Dunkerley, went into the vestry and announced to the choir that I was not expected to live out that night. Noon was so sure that I would not be alive in the morning that he took his surplice home with him, fully expecting that I should be dead and he would have to go to my funeral early on Monday. As it happened, I didn't die, but when waiting for news of me, Noon received a telegram from Bangkok bringing the startling news that the two great strong men we had played tennis with that day had gone off within twenty-four hours of each other, quite suddenly, with cholera! It was a fearful thing. You can imagine Noon's feelings. Out of that tennis four, two were dead and one had been given up by the doctors that day. He was the only one left and he wondered what was going to happen to him.

Well, yet one more recollection before I close this diary for good, and not a gruesome one this time.

I have mentioned the dance given to the *Albion*. We got very friendly with many of her fellows and at the dance, while sitting with the second lieutenant, a very jolly fellow, a man came up and, looking hard at him, said: 'Isn't your name so-and-so?' The second said he thought it was, at least he'd always been led to believe so. 'Well,' said the other man, 'you mayn't remember me, but you and I went up for our final on the *Britannia* together. You got through and I got plucked. That's close on fifteen years ago, and we haven't seen one another since; you joined the navy, I the Bombay Burmah Company. Have a drink.' They did, in fact they had several. The Bombay Burmah man, not being inured to hardships as was the man of the sea, got deliciously full! In fact, so muddled was he that when half past four in the morning came and Noon said we'd all go home and he'd drive us, the BB man mixed up our ponies with his old chum the officer. Mistaking them for him, he put his arms round their necks and swore he'd never, never, leave them. And I believe he wouldn't have done either if Noon hadn't climbed down from the box and threatened to horsewhip him if he didn't let go.

And then we started for home, with Noon on the box. Inside that small vehicle were the *Albion*'s pet commander (a model of discipline on board), the second luff, myself and two snotties, who came from no one knows where but who are always sure to be found if there is any fun going. Away we went then at full speed, leaving our poor syce, who wasn't expecting us to leave at that precise moment, to run yelling and screaming behind in a vain attempt to catch us.

Now, the turning to our hotel was a narrow lane and down

this Noon intended to turn. The ponies, however, considered they'd been out long enough and were determined to go home. Consequently there was a slight difference of opinion. Noon won, but not quite soon enough. He got his ponies round just as we had *passed* the turning, and took out a telegraph post stem on, so to speak, overturning the trap and precipitating us all very nicely into a three-foot drain which ran alongside the road. Naval men, however, have proverbially nine lives, and they must have lent us one each for the occasion for we got up none the worse for the spill. Seeing that the ponies and trap were all right, too, we made our way on foot to our various hotels, leaving the horses to the care of the syce who came up at the moment.

This tale has a sequel, also, but no moral.

Next morning the syce waited upon the naval men until about ten o'clock with a nice bill for damage to paint etc. Instead of paying it, they fired him down the stairs. He came up again, only to be kicked out once more. With a tenacity worthy of a better cause, he once more essayed to storm that staircase guarded by infuriated British naval officers, but with no better results than before. Then he went away for reinforcements. The naval men, thinking discretion the better part of valour, packed up and went off to their ship which was due to leave. When the syce came back again with help he found the birds had flown. He may be there yet for all I know, for we never saw him again.

We sailed from Bangkok for Singapore by the SS *Neun Tung*, a cargo boat of the North German Lloyd. The voyage was rough and uneventful, except for two things.

One day the captain, possibly because it was getting near Christmas, conceived the idea of having a shooting match. He possessed quite an armoury of rifles of various makes and sizes, and seemed to have ammunition for them all. So various targets, from bottles to whisky cases, were collected and thrown overboard, and we spent the morning—Noon, he and I—blazing away with the rifles and generally showing what bad shots we were. The ship was rolling heavily, so perhaps there was some excuse.

Then at night, after a good dinner, the captain voted for fireworks, and he there and then let off a large portion of the rockets that he carried. If anyone did that in the Gulf of Siam today they would probably find ships racing to their assistance, but in those days there were no ships, and the skipper, no doubt, was aware that he was perfectly safe in sending up the rockets.

The other matter to note was the fact that the skipper suddenly decided that he would arrive in Singapore on Christmas Eve instead of Christmas morning, and that we would all go to the Tingel Tangel together and have a good time!

In pursuit of this idea, and in order to get more speed out of his ship, he set sail! Yes, actually and definitely he rigged ship. With a full complement of sails and the engines going as hard as they could, we rolled down the Gulf of Siam, about the last steamboat to use sail as well as steam in those waters.

However, it was not to be, and we only arrived in Singapore early on Christmas morning. We landed from a sampan on Johnston's Pier at exactly seven o'clock, and with a rush home for a change managed to scramble back to the cathedral to take our places in the choir for the Christmas morning service.

And so ended my first trip to that very interesting city, Bangkok.

8

1903

The New Year of 1903 was to be an eventful one for me. I had returned from Bangkok feeling far from well, but with no definite symptoms of anything. I went to see the firm's doctor, a man called De Vos, and he gave me some medicine to take. He remarked at the same time that he would like to hear if it did me any good as he had been feeling the same way himself, and if the medicine did me good he would take some too! A good example of trying it on the dog!

The *Argonaut*, already mentioned in the last chapter, was still here, and one evening gave excellent entertainment on board to the Singapore public in return for hospitality received. Curiously enough, Captain Cherry was most affable that evening, greatly to the relief of the ship's company.

Admiral Keppel had slipped back to Singapore and was here at the beginning of the year, having wandered over to Port Said from the Riviera and joined a P&O boat there. He was, by this time, very frail indeed and, I was told, had come here hoping to die in the place!

News now came to hand that we were to be garrisoned once again by a white regiment, the 1st Battalion of the Manchesters, and they were expected to arrive about the end of March. More of them anon.

Another rickshaw strike occurred early in the year, but it was not nearly so serious as the one already referred to and was soon over. The sentences of the traffic court, presided over by Mr Hooper, were objected to and consequently a few discontented men—roughs, in fact, or to use their own word, *samseng*—set to work to terrorise the other pullers. A half-hearted affair altogether and soon over, but a nuisance while it lasted.

There were a lot of warships in Singapore at this time. In addition to the *Argonaut*, which was stationed here, HMS *Goliath* arrived, and then HMS *Glory*, flagship of the China Squadron, and attendant cruisers.

Sir Cyprian Bridge was a senior admiral, and his son was a midshipman on board. I got to know young Bridge fairly well, and had some good fun with him and his friends.

I am not sure but I think that that meeting of the admirals in 1903 was the beginning of the Singapore Naval Base.

My activities in Singapore were now to end for a considerable time. One night I became so ill that A.B. Cross and others decided that they would take me to hospital. They got a gharry and I suppose we arrived there, for I remember nothing much about it except that I was kept waiting in an office at the hospital while someone was found who would guarantee my hospital expenses. They say that I was kept waiting for over two hours, with a full dose of typhoid on me, and no doctor or nurse came to see what was the matter! That may or may not be true, but I was told the story afterwards. For myself, I came out of delirium about three weeks later to find a gentleman in clerical garb standing at my bedside. I said in a weak voice, 'Hello, Mr Dunkerley.' He replied in a very superior manner, 'Archdeacon now, if you please!' What else he said or what happened to him, I don't know, for off I went into another spell of delirium and came back to earth again about two weeks later!

The angel who undoubtedly saved my life was a Sister Knaggs, a splendid woman who knew more about the case than all the resident doctors put together. I know for a fact that she flatly refused to do things the doctors said. That I am alive today is, I am quite certain, solely due to her care and knowledge and good nursing. She herself used to say that my voice saved me, for I am told that I sang the Gilbert and Sullivan operas from end to end, going on without stopping, day and night throughout my delirium. As Sister Knaggs said, I never gave myself time to die.

I was in hospital for three months and three days altogether, a record up till then for a typhoid case. I came out of the place a skeleton with skin on!

It may perhaps be interesting to mention one or two things of importance that happened in the town during my illness, even though they cannot be said to be actually personal.

At Chinese New Year, the volunteer corps proceeded to camp at the same spot as before, namely what is now the Keppel Golf Course. The rain came down in torrents again and all accounts seem to show that it was a most miserable experience. The Chinese unit was in camp for the first time, and do not seem to have enjoyed the experience.

On 4 February 1903 Mr Buckley's great work, *An Anecdotal History of Singapore*, appeared from the printing press. This book is now out of print but it is a recognised book of reference and is being increasingly quoted, even in the law courts. It must have taken the old man many years to complete. Incidentally it led to the discovery of the original treaty of 6 February 1819, ceding Singapore to Britain. This document had been completely lost for many years, and hope had been given up of its recovery. Buckley, when hunting through old safes in the Johore Archives with the Dato Bintara Dalam—the only surviving son of Inche Abdulla (Malaya's historian)—came across the paper in a bundle of old documents. It was not written on parchment but on ordinary paper, and it is conjectured that Raffles had no parchment with him at the time. Two counterparts of the treaty were made. The one in the hands of English officialdom, with a staff of clerks and organisation, had been completely lost while, as Buckley says:

'The other, handed to a Malay chief who had not a chair, table, envelope or safe, had been carefully wrapped up, preserved and handed down through four generations and nearly a century of time.'

It was, of course, kept by the Temenggung of Singapore, and not by the Sultan of Johore.

There appears to have been more grousing among the cathedral congregation about this time. Some preacher had delivered a sermon from the pulpit in which he expressed the opinion that he did not consider it one of his first duties to visit his congregation.

Letters appeared in the papers upon the subject, and some of the remarks were bitter. There was, I am afraid, a good deal of truth in what was said.

The system of colonial chaplaincies was a wrong one, and it is now generally conceded that the government would have been wise if they had disestablished fifty years before they did. Chaplains were government servants and, unfortunately, there were times when this title counted more to them than their duties as ministers of God. Of course, such incidents were exceptions, and generally speaking the chaplains that have been appointed to Singapore have done their duty well. Nevertheless, the government servant system was wrong and the government did well to do away with it.

More trouble occurred at the theatre during the visit of the Brough company in February. It is a fact that the booking arrangements were very bad in those days, and this time things seem to have got to such a pass that a whole series of letters were written to the papers by people demanding apologies from others who had occupied their seats. Quite humorous to read nowadays, but no doubt the tempers of audiences that had to sit for hours cooped up in a hot steaming atmosphere, with no fans or *punkah*s, and the heat from hundreds of gas jets on the stage almost hitting them in the face, were rather tender, and liable to break out like this rather easily.

On 23 February the amateurs were at it again, this time with a production of R.C. Carton's *Liberty Hall*. I was, of course, out of it all, but I heard afterwards that it was a good show. It might have almost been called a Telegraph show because it was conceived and produced by Mr J.C.D. Jones, head of the cable depot. Mr A.Y. Gahagan, the general manager, played Briginshaw and Robert Binks was in the hands of Tommy Hose, the bishop's younger son, also in Telegraph employ.

But really the production was most notable, looking at it from this lapse of time, for the fact that it introduced to Singapore one of its greatest lady amateurs, Miss Maud Newton—now Mrs W.J. Mayson. She was given the part of Crafer, the vixenish servant girl, and made an instantaneous hit with it. Since then she has, in her time, played many parts, but I know that she has not forgotten that first appearance of hers, nor the success she made of her part.

The present-day motorist sometimes looks back upon the past and sighs for the days of horse-drawn vehicles, and the alleged safety of the roads in those days. There were, however, almost as many accidents then as now.

The Australian Waler horses that were used to draw the various kinds of conveyance were not always as well broken in as they might have been, and very often caused trouble.

There was a bad smash-up in Orchard Road in March of this year. The carriage of the GOC, General Sir A.F. Dorward, bolted in Orchard Road and ran into a trap driven by the late Mr T.O. Mayhew. The general was thrown out and sustained several injuries, while Mayhew's horse dashed into a tree and killed itself on the spot. Mayhew escaped unhurt, which was lucky.

The first Italian opera company to visit Singapore came at

the end of March. I can imagine what they must have had to put up with on the stage of the old town hall. They did their best, however, and tried to create an atmosphere by referring to the theatre on the programme as The Singapore Opera House.

The papers gave them fair notices, but finished up as follows:

'From an artistic point of view the season of the company is bound to be a success. From a financial one we are sorry to be unable to be equally prophetically optimistic.'

Evidently Singapore was living up to its reputation of being The Actor's Grave.

On their third appearance they played *La Bohème*. This was probably quite a new opera to the audience as a whole, and the paper, in its report, hoped sarcastically that the audience did not sit through the four acts in the hope of hearing 'When Other Lips', the favourite air from *The Bohemian Girl*. Evidently Singapore was not even then opera-minded.

I was by now convalescing. I was still in hospital, too weak to move, but the typhoid had left me and, fortunately, had left no ill effects in its train.

Indeed, nowadays I look back upon that illness as a blessing in disguise for it seemed to have acted as a spring cleaner to my body, clearing out of my system all the ills that, as a youth, I had suffered from. I had, in my short life, been in a bathchair for three separate and long periods; I had suffered from all kinds of ailments, including paralysis, and really I think that I started life after typhoid with a new body.

I remember well that first day Sister Knaggs said I could see a visitor. I asked her to ring up Mrs Abrams and to say that if she came would she bring me my mail. (Erny Abrams had been keeping my letters for me.)

In those days telephones in private houses were not as common as they are today, so Sister Knaggs rang up Daddy at the yard.

In due course dear Mrs Abrams drove up to the hospital laden down with jellies and fruits, chickens, etc., much to the surprise of the Sisters!

It appears that when Daddy got the message he mistook the word 'mail'. He rushed out into the yard, called Bertie Kirwan, his head stableman, pushed him on a horse and sent him galloping up to the Castle to Mrs Abrams with the message that she could go and see me. And, he added: 'For goodness' sake take him a good *meal*, the lad's starving.'

I was in hospital, too, when the Manchester Regiment, or rather its first battalion, arrived on 30 March, the first white battalion to be stationed in Singapore since the Second Boer War had broken out.

In those days the arrival of a new battalion was attended with much more picturesque ceremony than is the case today. There was, of course, no wheeled transport except bullock carts. In these used to be packed the women, children and the baggage, and a great procession would start from the docks, going along Kim Seng Road, Irwell Bank Road and Grange Road to the barracks. Having given this column sufficient time to get safely on its way, the new regiment would fall in on the wharf and, with bands playing, would set off on the march to Tanglin. In the meantime, the band and drums of the resident regiment would start out from the barracks, and the meeting place of official welcome was always the junction of Grange Road and Irwell Bank Road, where the band of the resident regiment would turn about and gaily play the new arrived one into barracks.

Next morning the ceremony would be reversed and would be one of goodbye.

The motor lorry and motor transport have changed all this, and a new regiment is now carried, lock, stock and barrel, to its destination in five-ton lorries.

The Manchester Regiment came here direct from South Africa. It had suffered severely in that campaign, and had been brought up to strength by a large batch of men recruited mainly from Liverpool Irishmen, a very tough lot!

If I remember rightly, the regiment did not earn a very good reputation here for behaviour; but also, I think, there were more teetotallers in the regiment than in most others.

It was a case of the good being very, very good, but when they were not they were horrid!

I was allowed to leave hospital after a sojourn there of three months and three days. Dear Mrs Abrams came and took charge of me, for I was still very, very weak. She drove me down to Katong, where the family were staying at the sultan's bungalow. I heard later that their visit to the seaside had been extended so that I might get the benefit of the fresh cool air. The Abrams were very, very good to me at that time, and if it had not been for their kindness in offering to take me and look after me during convalescence, I should have been kept in hospital for some weeks longer.

Towards the end of April I was considered strong enough to carry on on my own, and the firm decided to send me on a sea voyage to Shanghai to help with my recovery.

I left by P&O's SS *Bengal*, returning—after three weeks in the north—by the same steamer.

I went to Shanghai where I had friends, so had not to go to a hotel. During my three weeks' wait for the SS *Bengal* to return I took a trip to Japan, during which I had some interesting experiences which are well worth relating.

I started by experiencing the joys of typhoon weather on the way from Shanghai to Nagasaki, in a small ship of less than 2,000 tons. I do not want to go through the experience again.

I left the ship at Kobe and from there I visited, with some friends, the Osaka Exhibition. It was a wonderful experience. We were there on a day which was not a holiday, but was nevertheless one of the special days on which trips had brought in people from the more inaccessible parts of Japan. So I was privileged to see the Japanese people 'in the raw', so to speak, and very charming and unaffected I found them. I did not like the townspeople, if I remember rightly, but the country folk were delightful.

Osaka must be a very different city today from what it was in 1903. It seemed to consist then of long streets of one-storied wooden houses. We were met at the railway station by members of the Japanese Welcome Society, formed to look after foreign visitors to the exhibition, and they did us very well indeed. We were given rickshaws—for which we did not pay—and were sent for a ride round the town before going to the exhibition. At the show itself, free passes for everything were showered courteously.

We were, I think, the only Europeans in the exhibition that day. When we—there were four of us—decided to go down the water chute, all other traffic was stopped and we were made a show of for the benefit of the country folk, many of whom, I was told, had never seen Europeans before.

There was one very fine erection in the exhibition, I remember, which was the highest there and could be seen from many miles away. It took the form of an up-ended beer barrel. There was a staircase outside it, starting from the ground and running spirally round the barrel until it finished at the bunghole. We watched the people going up these stairs. They looked like flies, so high up were they, so we decided to investigate ourselves.

We entered the bunghole in due course and found ourselves in a vast sanded-floor beer hall where we were given some of the most delicious light beer I have ever tasted. It was, I think, Asahi. After that climb up, and in the wonderful cool air that blew through the room, it tasted like nectar, or at all events how I feel nectar ought to taste like.

It was while staying in Kobe after my friends had gone on that I noticed the arrival of a British cruiser, which turned out to be the *Argonaut*. I took a boat and went off to her. I was fortunate to catch my friend Candy just leaving for a few days on shore. He went back with me and we had a very delightful time together, doing various trips and seeing much of the local countryside, though I couldn't get very far as I was still feeling the effects of my illness.

We visited a very big tea house one evening, and paid our money for some geisha to dance for us. To me it was very interesting and amusing.

I had played in the great success, *The Geisha*, on two occasions before leaving England: once in the chorus, and later on in the lead part of Fairfax. I had very little thought then of ever seeing a real geisha in the flesh.

In the tea house I had great fun. I was acquainted with the Japanese instrument the *shamisen*, on which I used to strum during rehearsals. So I took an instrument from one of the girls and played 'We won't go home till morning'. I also sang for them the Japanese songs from *The Geisha* and *The Mikado*. Remembering the goodbye business between Molly and the Marquis in the former, I taught it to the girls, to their huge delight. In case it isn't remembered, I will describe it briefly. The Marquis and Molly kneel opposite each other, then solemnly bow their heads to the ground, first to the right and then to the left. Molly, of course, then slaps the face of the Marquis with her fan and runs off. I wonder how many visitors were greeted, after my visit, in this fashion?

I also visited the big Japanese theatre in Kobe—not the one run on European lines but the real national affair. It was peculiarly interesting to me, and I made copious notes about it at the time. We paid our entrance fee at a desk in the street which was, I suppose, the local equivalent of the box office, and went in.

There were no chairs in the theatre. The whole of the ground floor was divided up into little squares, rather like low sheep pens measuring about four feet across. In each square there seemed to be a little charcoal stove for warming food. These stoves seemed to be provided by the management, probably at a small extra charge.

At the back of the theatre was a gallery, and at the sides were raised platforms, divided again into boxes. We took one of these, which were more expensive than the pit pens. In view of our nationality chairs were brought us, otherwise we would have had to sit on the floor.

The stage itself fascinated me. There was a curtain, a modern concession, but it was some distance back from the front of the stage.

The dressing rooms must have been at the end of the theatre opposite the stage, for the entrances and exits were made along a raised platform that ran right down one side of the pit and was the same height as the stage.

On either side of the stage itself were two raised platforms. On one of these the reader of the story knelt, with his big storybook in front of him, and on the other knelt the orchestra (two men who seemed to occupy their time by hitting a wooden board with two pieces of wood shaped like bricks!)

Ancient Japanese plays are all in mime. The talking is done by the reader, who has a most expressive way of delivering the story. In this he is assisted by the orchestra who, by means of crescendos

169

and diminuendos, give wonderful emphasis to the words.

The acting seemed to begin the moment an actor stepped onto the raised platform, and sometimes it took quite a long time before the stage was reached and the platform was clear for another actor to make his appearance.

The light for all this by-play on the platform was provided by a gentleman clothed completely in black, who carried a very long piece of bamboo with a lit candle at the end. The footlight man was masked, and was supposed to be invisible. His manipulation of the quaint footlight was extraordinarily clever.

All the scene-shifters, too, walked about in black and were masked, like the footlight man. They carried on their duties of moving scenery while the play was going on and in full view of the audience, only one is not supposed to be able to see them.

I should have mentioned that in the orchestra there was one man playing a *shamisen*, who keept up a sort of humming sound while the reading was going on. The music was rather like a series of Gregorian tones.

When a scene ended and the curtain came down, every little nipper in the theatre—and there were crowds of children there— jumped up onto the stage platform. They started sliding up and down it, running onto the stage and disporting themselves merrily until the next scene was due and they were driven back to their pens by footlights.

It also seemed to be quite the thing for the older people to get up onto the stage and peep under the bottom of the curtain!

I wonder what Mr Cochran would say if some of his London

audiences developed this habit?

In due course I left Kobe for Shanghai, again by steamer. Anchoring at Moji, I and another passenger decided to go on shore. First we went to Shimonoseki, opposite Moji, and had a look round. We saw the temple where Li Hongzhang signed the treaty of peace after the first Sino–Japanese war.

Then we went across the straits to Moji and, coming back from there in a sampan, the boatman stopped and demanded double fare. My notes made at the time show that we had to take the seat planks to him before he could be induced to continue. When we got to the ship he was so insistent in demanding more money that we had to throw him down the gangway. The captain said it was fortunate that we were sailing at once as otherwise we might have got into trouble over the incident.

We went ashore again at Nagasaki, which struck me as being very picturesque, and very like the storybook pictures of Japan. At that time very few Europeans lived there—less than one hundred, I was told—and the principal trade seemed to be woodcarving.

We climbed the numberless steps of the famous temple, and duly admired the view from the top. As I was looking at the big bronze horse from which the temple takes its name, a Japanese came up to me and, with a most polite bow, said:

'Allow me to introduce myself. For many years I have been a certified guide, and very well know this place. I think if you go by yourself round about you will not understand, and then I think the trouble will be very damn!'

His services were not utilised, but I made a note of the speech at the time as it amused me very much.

From Nagasaki we crossed to China, meeting rough weather again, but we arrived in the Woosung River without mishap.

Shanghai was a very different place in 1903 from what it is today. To begin with, it was very much smaller. The Greater Shanghai of modern days did not exist, and the concession ended at the Bubbling Well. Here, there was a place of entertainment just outside municipal jurisdiction where gambling and much more dangerous vices were rampant. No control could be kept over the place as it was in Chinese territory proper and I understand that, at times, it caused considerable trouble to the authorities.

The French concession existed then, as now, and on the other side of the town the American Quarter was just beginning to spring up.

I suppose the Bund must look very different today from what it did then. The old club has given place to a new one, and possibly that is a pity for that old club was one of the most comfortable places of its kind that I have ever been in. I have very pleasant recollections of cosy afternoon snoozes in a comfortable armchair in front of a nice fire in the library, followed by a very acceptable cup of tea. Everyone met at the club bar before tiffin—no doubt they do today—but the place was much smaller then, and possibly one's circle of acquaintances was larger. I was told that the place was used as a sort of exchange and that a lot of business was done there.

I stayed with an old friend from Manchester, whose sister I was afterwards to marry. He was a member of the Shanghai Light

Horse, so I saw a lot of the activities of that celebrated corps, as I did also of Shanghai's pride, its Volunteer Fire Brigade. Billings, who had lived with me in Singapore, was a member of the Mih Ho Lung division, and lived in the mess above the fire station. The brigade was very smart and was kept very up to date. I was present at an annual inspection, and was very much impressed with all I saw.

I did not do much in Shanghai as before I went to Japan I wasn't fit for much exertion. When I came back I had to leave for Singapore almost immediately, but I drove round the streets a good deal and, short of entering the Chinese city, got a very good knowledge of the geography of the settlement.

I suppose that if I ever go there again I shall find that all the old landmarks have entirely disappeared.

Shortly after my return from Japan I left Shanghai by the SS *Bengal* and, in due course, arrived in Singapore fully restored to health and strength again.

9

Back in Singapore, and at work again after my long illness and my trip to China, I took up my life again with a certain feeling of strangeness. Whitefields were full and therefore, as I could not go back there, I went into residence again at the Hotel de la Paix.

There I met for the first time a Mr Pringle, who was representing the YMCA and was in Singapore with the intention of forming a branch here. I never liked Pringle. He used to take it upon himself to lecture me when he found that I went to church on a Sunday morning and then sometimes went to the office. He was full of Biblical quotations which he thought suitable to the occasion, and altogether annoyed me very much. Possibly Pringle set me against the YMCA as a whole, for I have never had much faith in it or in the work that it was supposed to do here.

I left the hotel after about six weeks, and together with John Robertson, 'Algy' Langley and W.W. MacMillan—all men who are well remembered today in Singapore—started a mess at Waverley, a house just outside the compound of Boustead's big house at the top of Orchard Road.

It was a house very much in favour with young men starting

housekeeping. Many celebrated messes started life there, and it was cheap and easy to run. We were a happy four, and lived together in good fellowship and harmony until home leave broke up the combine. I shall have more to say about Waverley and its inmates later on.

On Friday, 24 July SVC's annual meeting was held. The SVR was still holding together, but the threads of existence were getting very slender. The CO—at this time Major Broadrick—in his opening remarks said that he could not congratulate the corps on the year's working. Only sixty SVRs had made themselves efficient, and that unit had distinguished itself at the annual inspection by the fact that not a single one of its many sergeants had taken the trouble to put in an appearance. A sorry state of affairs.

Of course, there was more than one reason for the bad condition of the corps. The treatment meted out to the coronation contingent—not by the home authorities, but by its own officers—had been little short of scandalous, and though the complaints were hushed up and never got into print, they were common property. It would not be right for me to rake up old troubles of this description, nor is it my purpose to write of matters that did not touch me personally, but I met, as others did, the returned members of the contingent and heard all the stories, humorous and the reverse, which they had to tell. The accounts did not reflect with credit upon the commissioned ranks, and had a very harmful effect upon volunteering as a whole.

As a matter of fact, volunteering in the Settlement had reached such an unhealthy state that the movement could have been classed as very sick indeed, and likely to expire at any moment. Numerous letters appeared in the paper venting various grievances, and alleging breaches of good taste and military etiquette among the commissioned and non-commissioned officers. Finally the papers themselves were drawn into the trouble and, if proof were needed that there was justification for the complaints made, it was forthcoming in *The Straits Times* on 31 July. That paper stated that, during the visit of the SVC to England at the time of the coronation, a member of the staff of this paper was on more than one occasion summoned before his commanding officer, though certainly never actually punished, on account of letters which he did *not* write, but which appeared in *The Straits Times*.

The fact of the matter was that the commissioned ranks were, as a whole, thoroughly incompetent, and were trying all they knew to cover up their lack of knowledge by bullying and bluff.

It seems rather hard to say this, but my own personal knowledge is confirmed by the papers of the day.

A mild sort of mutiny took place in the form of a round robin, which was supposed to be for Volunteers only but which the whole town, including the newspapers, had knowledge of. Its purport was to force the commanding officer to call a general meeting to enquire into the reasons for the alleged unpopularity of the corps.

Senior officers also wrote to the papers asking if the names of the writers of other letters could be given to them, a request which the papers very rightly refused.

Altogether the position was becoming almost intolerable, and it was not long before a shake-up took place.

All this, however, did not prevent us from turning out for field days, and on August bank holiday we had a very interesting morning.

The general idea of the scheme was that the enemy—composed of the 13th Madras Infantry, the Malay States Guides, the SVI and SVR—had landed on the north of the island and were attaching the docks with the object of destroying the coal sheds. The advance was made in two columns, the regulars coming from the direction of Pasir Panjang while the Volunteers attacked from the Serangoon side.

We moved off from the racecourse about half past five in the morning, taking Government House—where we metaphorically cut the telephone by signing our names and the time—and moved off towards Fort Canning.

I had charge of a section and was sent via Killiney Road, the idea being to surround the fort. It was pointed out that if we were seen before we got into position, the attack would be considered a failure. When we got to the top of Killiney Road, after dealing faithfully with the telephone and telegraph in the post office in Orchard Road, we were thirsty. So we decided to cut the telephone at Waterloo Mess where Gilfillan Wood's men were housed. It was a famous mess in its day, standing at the corner of Killiney and River Valley Roads.

The drinks were welcome, and good. Then came the difficulty of getting down River Valley Road hill without being seen from the fort, an obvious impossibility on foot. It was then that I had a brainwave. I collected all the rickshaws I could find (they were bigger then than now), put two men in each, pulled up the hood and fastened the apron as high as possible. I sent them off at intervals with instructions to keep hood and apron up till they got to the corner of Hill Street.

And so I got my men onto the slopes of Fort Canning without mishap. Here we found others of the SVR, among them old Mr Lloyd, the auctioneer, known as Pa to distinguish him from the other equally famous Daddy Abrams.

Old Lloyd was way above volunteering age, but was very keen and wouldn't miss a field day if he could help it. To enable himself to last he made careful preparations, and a rickshaw and two of his office assistants were always within reach. Ostensibly they were there to carry him off the field when he gave in but, being a sensible man, he filled the rickshaw with a box of ice and drinks in case he didn't want to use it as an ambulance.

And here we all were, lying out on the slopes of Fort Canning, just under the lip of the moat, being served with iced *stengah*s by two Malay boys. Even the much-maligned volunteering had its pleasant moments!

We took Fort Canning from the other side, at least the Eurasian company did while we were having refreshments, and then we moved off to the docks.

At the Tanjong Pagar police station we found a picket of the Manchester Regiment, who weren't going to move for any bloody Volunteers, so an argument occurred. It ended when a corporal of the Manchester Regiment laid his rifle down in the road and invited his argumentative opponent to 'Come on!' The challenge was promptly accepted, and a very nice little scrap had developed when the words 'Cease fire!' sounded.

Oh! I forgot to mention that just prior to the argument we had captured the Boustead Institute and drunk their beer.

The other column had a scrap of a different nature, which resulted in the cease-fire being sounded before the operations ended. Either the 13th Madrassies or the MSG on the one hand, or the Manchesters on the other, had gone for their opponents with the bayonet and wounded three men.

This did *not* get into the paper.

Still, volunteering had its moments, even in those days of corps sickness.

As an interesting sidelight upon the methods of keeping records at the drill hall in those days, to which I have already referred in an earlier chapter, it is amusing to note another event. On 7 August the Volunteers suddenly woke up to my existence, and corps orders on that date graciously announced that 'Private E.A. Brown is taken on the strength of the SVR from 28 July 1903.' I suppose that up to that time they must have thought I was still in the SVA which I had never joined.

To turn from tales of playing at war to the real thing, the many rumours regarding trouble between Russia and Japan were rapidly crystallising into a very serious situation. We in Singapore could not help taking a great interest in what was going on, and little sidelights on the frantic preparations being made by both sides for war kept showing themselves.

One day a Jew walked into the godown and purchased, at a very high price, my whole stock of scarlet woollen blankets which had been lying immovable for a long time. He was, of course, acting as agent for a Japanese firm.

All sorts of idle stocks were got rid of at this time by the big importers, and so in a roundabout way we benefited.

The question as to whether the Russian Fleet would be sent out, or whether the war would be wholly fought on land, was fiercely debated. The general opinion was that if it did come out, it would be met by the Japs somewhere in the region of Singapore. Subsequent events showed that we were wrong, but the idea made things more interesting for the people in the Straits.

The last expiring flicker of life in the SVR showed up at the end of August when the unit, under its OC, Captain Elliot, made a valiant effort to pull itself together, get in recruits and start being a good boy again. The effort was not to prove successful, however.

In September I was singing again in public, making my first appearance after my illness at a Philharmonic Orchestral Concert, where I sang a song that is still a great favourite of mine, 'The Devout Lover'. I wonder if any love song has ever been quite so popular as this; it never fails to please.

A little note in the papers about this time states the bald fact that: 'Miss Jackson and Miss Hands, the two lady typists engaged by ..., left for Sydney yesterday by the SS *Salazie*. It is understood that they were sent back by the colonial authorities.'

It would be perhaps indiscreet on my part to detail the drama that lies behind this bald announcement in the papers, but I met the two ladies in question and exceedingly nice girls they were. They were met, on arrival from Australia, by government authorities. One, at all events, was lodged at St Mary's Home until arrangements could be made for their return to the homes in Australia which they had unfortunately left.

On 17 September it was decided, at a meeting presided over by Sir Frank Swettenham, to alter the style of building of the Memorial Hall—which had now been hanging fire for some time, and to proceed on the lines of new plans drawn up by Mr Bidwell of Swan & McLaren. Though the governor's speech was carefully worded it was easy to see that there had been some bad blundering on the part of the PWD. They had, in fact, prepared a model of the proposed building in order to induce public subscriptions, without having any working plans. In fact, the governor stated: 'He believed—although he spoke subject to contradiction—that they had not all been made even at the time the meeting was held.' Bidwell's plans were accepted, and from that date the erection of the building went on apace.

At a special meeting of the SVC held about this date to try and induce a little enthusiasm, no new facts came to light. Volunteering was 'silly', 'not enough exercise in it', 'no military knowledge among the officers and NCOs', etc., etc. were the complaints. However, everyone promised to do their best and matters were smoothed over for a time.

Then the poor old band came in for a good wigging. Volunteers were supposed to pay fifty cents a month for its upkeep. It was accused of being 'no good', of never turning up when wanted; of appearing in all kinds of uniform or no uniform at all; of parading—when it *did* parade—in white sandshoes; of splitting itself up into little parties to play at Chinese funerals, in fact of everything wicked that could be thought of.

And the municipal subscription to it was S$6,000 per annum. Today, for the sum of S$10,000, the municipality have the complete services of a magnificent police band which plays three times a week in the public parks. It is conducted by a British Army bandmaster, Mr Minns, well known in his profession, late of the Sussex Regiment—and there are those who think that value is not being obtained for the money. Think of these facts, ye doubting present-day commissioners, and compare them with your predecessors' idea of value.

A somewhat celebrated lady pianist passed through Singapore and gave a concert on 21 September. Various amateurs helped her, I among them. I sang Florence Aylward's 'Love's Coronation', accompanied by piano, violin and 'organ'. I mention this fact because the organ was a harmonium, played by Mr Salzmann. If I sang the song today, I would be accompanied on a magnificent three-manual organ belonging to the public and erected in their splendid concert room in the Memorial Hall.

We have indeed progressed since old Mr Salzmann accompanied me on a harmonium which the papers dignified by the name of organ.

About this time I began bowling again with some success,

and possess a mug dated 1903. It was won with my messmate Johnny Robertson, in the professional pairs at the SCC Autumn Tournament that year.

We played croquet in those days, too, but only among the best people. As the Ladies' Lawn members were considered to be in this class, tournaments used to be played there and they attracted quite large entries.

On Sunday, 4 October I made my first journey on the recently opened Singapore–Kranji Railway, starting from Tank Road Station at about half past five in the morning in an open truck! It was the occasion of a field day at Holland Road and the authorities were testing the railway as a military asset, I presume.

Does anyone remember that a sea serpent once appeared in Singapore harbour? It was reported to have been seen near the old hulks at the entrance to Tanjong Pagar by one of the Marine Police officers. And in case anyone ever compiles a fresh history of this mythical sea monster, the date of its appearance here was Saturday evening, 10 October 1903.

Lots of funny things were found in the sea in those days. Soon after the appearance of the sea serpent, a huge turtle was caught in the river at Cavenagh Bridge. It was seen crawling about in the mud at low water and, curiously enough, one of the two Marine Police officers who captured it—with the help of a tennis net and after a lively struggle—was the same man who had seen the sea serpent the previous Saturday!

For some time now rehearsals for *The Yeomen of the Guard* had been going on apace. The little coterie of gentlemen who had been so successful with their *Pinafore* production, and whose faith in youth had been so splendidly justified in that opera, had decided to continue the good work.

As the gentlemen in question were really the forerunners of the later famous Singapore Amateur Dramatic Committee, it will be well to mention their names here. The three principals were Messrs W.A. Dowley (of the Vacuum Oil Co.), F.W. Barker (a broker, afterwards head of the rubber firm bearing his name) and E.F.H. Edlin (a partner in Drew & Napier). There were, of course, others but the real work was done, and interest sustained, by these three.

Again they pinned their faith on the younger set, except for the musical side of the production which they put in the safe hands of Mr E. Salzmann. The one lady member of the cast who did not definitely come under the heading of young was Mrs Hooper, but she was an experienced actress with a fine deep contralto voice, and fitted her part of Dame Carruthers splendidly. Mrs Hooper was one of a trio of three sisters, well known in Malaya. The other two married Sir W. Birch and Mr Justice Ebden respectively. All three were handsome, but perhaps Mrs Hooper took the palm in this direction, and in addition had an excellent stage presence and knew how to walk. I think I can say, without exaggeration, that she was the best amateur Gilbert and Sullivan 'heavy contralto' that I have ever met.

The committee in this production decided to go one better than they had done in *Pinafore*. They decided to choose a producer also from among the youngsters. Their choice fell on me. A man called Criswick (of the Borneo Company), with a nice baritone voice, took the part of Lieutenant of the Tower, which would otherwise have fallen to my lot.

And so there came into my life a new activity which fascinated me and which was to provide me, for many years, with a very delightful and interesting occupation. I was now a producer! And very proud I was of the fact, I can assure you.

I had watched the methods of the various producers and stage managers I had played with, and had made up my mind that when, if ever, I got my chance, I would introduce some drastic changes. Not necessarily changes in the methods on the stage, but in the 'unwritten laws' that surrounded rehearsals at that time.

Two, in particular, had always seemed to me absurd. One was the habit of coming to rehearsals in evening dress.

Up to this time no one had ever dared to come to rehearsal in old clothes and, as a consequence, sitting down on the stage in the course of a rehearsal was not to be thought of. I introduced the 'sitting down' effect for the first time in 'I have a song to sing O' and informed the cast that evening dress was done away with and old clothes would be the rule in future.

One lady in the chorus refused to believe that I really dared to be iconoclastic, and came to the next rehearsal in evening dress— a nice black lace one, I remember. Being so clad, she refused to sit down on the dirty stage and had to stand up by herself. But fate played into my hands that night for, later on, when dancing round in another chorus movement, the wire netting over the gas footlights caught that nice black lace and literally ripped the skirt off the lady!

And after that old clothes became the fashion.

Another fetish that caused trouble but which I insisted on altering was the presence of hangers-on behind the scenes.

The stage door Johnny still existed at that time, in amateur as well as in professional circles. One acquired merit if one could, in some way or other, manage to be behind while a show was going on. Sometimes there were more outsiders in the wings than performers on the stage. And the amount they cost the shows in free drinks!

And so I stopped it, and definitely refused to allow followers behind the scenes or into rehearsals, a rule that I have rigidly adhered to from that day to this, and in which I have been loyally backed up always by both cast and committee.

On the King's birthday, 10 November of this year, a curious thing happened, and is well worth recording.

The usual parade of troops took place in the morning, but none of the SVC, with the exception of the SVA who fired the salute, were present!

The official reason given for the absence of the corps was that it was engaged in field manoeuvres elsewhere, but that is such a weak excuse that it can hardly have been the real reason. It is a pity that I cannot remember the facts because I am sure that they would be extremely interesting to Volunteers today. I wonder what would happen if the SVC were told nowadays that they were not wanted on the King's birthday parade! I expect that the reason at the time was that the corps was so terribly bad at drill that it would have been unsafe to parade it!

A very versatile gentleman made his first bow to a Singapore audience at a Philharmonic concert on 13 November in the person of a Mr Valois, a Belgian. Valois had come out to one of the smaller German firms, and what he couldn't do with a cello wasn't worth knowing. He was by far the most brilliant player of a stringed instrument that the Singapore amateurs have produced, even to the present day, and that is saying a very great deal. Withal he was such a delightful fellow, so willing to help in anything and so full of fun that he became a very great favourite. It was said of him that if one left a bow and an old box lying about, Valois would have a playable instrument ready for use in half an hour! Certainly his collection of weird and wonderful fiddles was amazing. His favourite one was made out of a broom handle and a four-gallon Devoe's old tin.

I was told that when he left Singapore and went to London he played as an amateur in the Queen's Hall Orchestra, but of this I am not sure.

A very old-established Singapore firm, Messrs Puttfarcken & Co., suspended payment on 18 November of this year. Their partner in the East, Mr Theodore Sohst, had been, at one time, the German consul in Singapore. He was a very courtly representative of the old-type German, and those who remember the older generation of Germans in the East thirty years ago will know what I mean. The younger generation then coming out were beginning to show signs of that so-called Kultur that was afterwards to lead the nation to disaster, but the older men were very fine gentlemen indeed.

Messrs Puttfarcken & Co. was one of the oldest of the German firms here, having been established as long ago as 1858, or almost immediately after Singapore broke away from India and became a crown colony. Their headquarters were in Hamburg.

While on the subject of the Germans it is worthwhile recording that the third son of the Kaiser, Prince Adalbert, then eighteen years of age, passed through Singapore on his way to join the German China Squadron as a midshipman. There was tremendous excitement among the German community and especially among the ladies, who were all anxious to be introduced to him and to say they had spoken to him. The wife of my immediate head in the import department, a Mrs Olsen, was considerably disliked for a long time afterwards because, being young and pretty—a somewhat rare thing in the community—the prince had spent most of the time at the evening reception at the club in her company! I remember the occasion and the lady well, and don't blame the prince in the slightest.

The Presbyterian Church members, under the ministry of Mr Walker, were much divided in opinion about this time as to the advisability or not of changing the hour of afternoon service. The usual time had been a quarter to five, and Walker proposed altering it to half past five. Listen to this, you churchgoers who sit in comfort under your fans and electric lights. This is an extract from a letter written to the papers by a gentleman calling himself Rothesay, and it gives I think a good insight into the conditions of life prevailing in Singapore in the year 1903.

'The hour of a quarter to five has distinct advantages over the other hours mentioned, especially in a poorly ventilated building which, with lights [gas] full on, is apt to become—notwithstanding *punkah*s—unpleasantly close and oppressive. A service terminating at six o'clock enables those attending it to return home before dark or, if they prefer it, to have a pleasant half-hour's airing and still be home in good time for the seven o'clock dinner.'

On Saturday, 12 December the amateurs made their bow to the public in *The Yeomen of the Guard*. The papers were again kind to us, and as a matter of fact the whole performance was well ahead of the previous opera, *HMS Pinafore*. Here are some extracts from *The Straits Times*, in a *real* criticism which did not hesitate to point out the faults and places where improvements might be effected:

'For an amateur first night it was a veritable triumph of management, as the piece was carried through without a hitch from the overture to the drop.'

'Spectacularly the performance was one of the most magnificent ever given in Singapore.'

'It was a very excellent orchestra, as good as could be produced by any settlement in the East.'

'The chorus also merits especial commendation, it was especially well trained, and remarkably picturesque.'

As a matter of fact there was some really good acting in the production. E.E. (Bill) Sykes of Gilfillan Wood gave a magnificent rendering of the part of Shadbolt, as good a one as

I ever remember seeing; Billy Dunman was as reliable as ever in Jack Point, and his final scene and death was excellently done. Mrs Hooper in the part of Dame Carruthers was excellent.

Altogether the production can be said to have been another step up the ladder that was to lead Singapore to the position which it afterwards held in the realm of amateur opera in the East.

About the middle of December a most curious affair took place. For some reason or other it was rumoured in Chinatown that those two hereditary enemies, the Macau and Fuzhou factions, were to fight out their grievances, with the sanction of the authorities, in a pitched battle on the esplanade. The government would provide police to see fair play, and 'for this occasion only' life would be as it used to be 'in the good old days' in China, with broken heads for trophies and damaged carcasses for luck.

Sure enough, by one o'clock on Monday, 14 December an immense crowd had begun to collect on the esplanade. All the riffraff of the town were there: the *tongkang* and *twakow* men; the coolies from the riverside godowns; the ragtag and bobtail that go to make up the scum of Singapore's Chinese population, all were converging on the esplanade.

Then out came the police. 'There, what did we tell you?' said the knowing ones. 'Here's proof that the government are going to help us enjoy ourselves.'

And when the Sikh police began, in a bored way, to get the crowd off the esplanade, starting from the centre and working outwards, it looked as if the rumour was correct and the arena was being cleared for the fight.

So the crowd, now between 10,000 and 15,000 strong, moved off the ground onto the roads. The police made a ring round the alleged battleground, and the Chinese crowd very sportingly conceding the right of the combatants to a clear field.

The police looked bored. It was a long wait but the crowd, quite contented and happy, sat down and amused themselves until the kick-off time, fixed for four o'clock in the afternoon, arrived.

Four o'clock came, no combatants appeared and the police yawned and woke up. Gradually, without haste and with no obvious effort, they shepherded that huge crowd farther and farther away. People on the outskirts began to go home, others followed and by six o'clock there was nothing to be seen of what might have been an extremely serious affair. The behaviour and tactics of the police were excellent—they joked with the crowd, kept them in good humour and let time do the work for them.

The origin of the rumour that caused this most curious affair does not seem to have been discovered.

The SVR was now being laid out for its funeral. Circulars had been sent round the members informing them that the corps was to be disbanded and asking whether they would sign on in the SVA, SRE (V) or go on the reserve.

It was recognised that the unit was dead, and all that was now required was a decent funeral. That came in a few days, and at the beginning of 1904 the old SVR became a thing of the past. A few die-hards, of whom I was one, refused to resign or transfer and we were left in the air.

We maintained that we had joined the SVC and that the corps

could not kick us out. Infantrymen we were and infantrymen we intended to remain. We used to regularly turn up at the drill hall on what had been drill nights, get ourselves marked on the roll as being present and then go on our way.

The difficulty was solved later with the aid of the SVA Maxim Guns, but more of that anon.

War was now definitely in the air, and it would only be a matter of days before the inevitable happened, and Japan and Russia broke off relations. At the end of the year, however, negotiations were still going on and the break hadn't come.

The vexing question of the fire brigade was now about to be settled. G.P. Owen, the chief of the brigade, was going on leave and asked to be relieved of his duties on account of age. It was definitely resolved to ask Messrs Merryweather & Co., the makers of fire engines, to pick a suitable man to be head of the Singapore brigade. In due course Mr Pett, already referred to, arrived in Singapore to fill the post.

The Yeomen of the Guard had made positively its last appearance, but then decided to give two more performances after Christmas. It had played to crowded houses throughout its run, and still the audiences were not satisfied. Like Oliver Twist, they asked for more, so it was decided to satisfy them.

And so the year came to an end, a year that had been an eventful one in my life and in which I had seen more of the East than I'd ever expected to.

10

1904

The beginning of another year, my fourth in Singapore and the last one of my first contract. I had thoroughly 'dug myself in' to Singapore by now, and was fully determined to stay on in the place if the firm offered me another contract. I was happy, was in a nice mess with congenial messmates and life in the East seemed to suit me. I had, by this time, quite got over my severe illness. In fact it seemed to have done me good, and to have driven out of my system all the ill health that I had been accustomed to in my early youth. Typhoid so often leaves some disaster behind it; in my case the opposite had occurred, and for the first time in my young life I was feeling really fit and healthy.

Present-day members of the SAFA (Singapore Amateur Football Association) will be interested to learn that early in January of 1904, the first attempt was made to form a football league. A meeting was called at the YMCA to discuss the matter, and the suggestion was adopted. About twelve teams, mostly European, were enrolled. The exceptions were the SVI (Volunteer Infantry), the YMCA and John Little & Company, the last two proposing to put mixed teams on the field. Here, therefore, is the beginning of the entry of the Asiatic into football circles, a move which was to go from strength to strength and lead to the Asiatic football teams of today which are numbered in their hundreds.

Those who did not know the local-born before they took to playing European open-air games can appreciate the good in general health and stamina that this move has done. I am certain in my own mind that football can be given the credit for the great improvement in the general physique of the local-born that is so very noticeable today.

Gilbert and Sullivan enthusiasts will be horrified to hear that at the last performance of *The Yeomen of the Guard*, topical verses were introduced by Billy Dunman into the duet 'Cock and Bull'. It seems terrible to write today that this happened, but perhaps thirty years ago the veneration for the words of the immortal Gilbert was not as great as it is nowadays. One of the verses is interesting, as it shows the trend of the movement concerning the exchange:

> 'When exchange bobs up and down,
> Then we holler for a dollar,
> That is fixed at half a crown
> Or a shilling if you're willing,
> And they tell us every day
> We'll have fixity in this big city
> Before the month of May
> Sterling basis—smiling faces etc., etc.'

Pretty crude, you'll say, but the verse and others like it were reported to have brought down the house.

Single-seated rickshaws appeared for the first time in January 1904. They were said to be 'very smart-looking, rubber-tyred vehicles and single-seated'. Up to this time the rickshaws had been iron-tyred and all doubled-seated, with a wider beam than those known as double-seaters today, which are really a compromise between the old double-seater and the single rickshaw. It is said that Sir Arthur Young, when he was governor, saw two fat chitties sitting in a rickshaw pulled by an emaciated coolie proceeding up Government Hill. He thereupon made a suggestion to abolish the double rickshaw altogether. It was pointed out that this would react harshly on parents who had more than one child to send to school. So a compromise was effected, the double rickshaw being reduced in size so that while it would accommodate two children, the two fat chitties, or their equivalent, would have to take one apiece.

'Forty-five miles in a motorcar.' There's a heading for a newspaper article that should thrill you. Anyhow, it was thought well enough of to devote a whole column of *The Straits Times* to a description of the trip, which was from Kuala Kubu to Raub and which started thuswise:

'Many people in Singapore hardly realise the pleasures and excitements obtainable in a tour into the Malay States, that has become possible since the advent of the French Automobile Company etc., etc.'

Excitement? Yes, certainly. Pleasures? I wonder!

Oh, and listen to this, too:

'So great is the skill of the chauffeurs that at a moment's notice they can bring the car to a dead stop, thus avoiding bullock carts at corners.'

There's driving skill for you!

As I have mentioned before, theatrical companies of all sorts used to pass through Singapore and some of them, alas, got no farther.

One such was the Hill Company which disintegrated here, leaving a very charming singer, a Miss Marjorie Tempest, to do the best she could for herself. She was not actually of the company, but had been on a concert tour, and had been taken on by them to vary their show a bit.

Several of us helped her in a very successful concert which we got up for her in the town hall. Among other things Billy Dunman, she and I sang that celebrated old trio, 'Memory'. Billy and I also sang the duet from *Cox and Box*.

A telegram from London on 18 January announced the death of Admiral Sir Harry Keppel, about whom I have already had occasion to write.

Sir Frank Swettenham, the governor, had gone home on leave and Sir William Taylor had been acting in his place. On 23 January it was announced that Sir John Anderson, of the colonial office, had been appointed governor of the Straits Settlements. Nothing was known about him in Singapore, and as he was said to have had no colonial experience whatsoever, speculation was rife as to how he would fit the post. If I remember rightly, the appointment was not a popular one; there were many then, as there are today, who strongly objected to outsiders being given the plums of the Malayan Civil Service (or the Straits Settlements Civil Service as it was then). And so the man who was destined to be one of our greatest governors began his appointment in an atmosphere that was not altogether friendly towards him.

At the same time, and actually on the same day as the telegram arrived, the salary of the governor was raised by the Legislative Council to £6,000 per annum 'of which £1,200 was to be considered as an entertainment allowance'.

We had the cinematograph again this month at the town hall, in the charge of two gentlemen who had exhibited it in 'various parts of the world'.

It was not a success! The manager wrote to the papers and explained that the fault was due to the bad light, and this in turn was due to the damp weather affecting the lime sticks, causing them to crumble and break. Sounds funny these days, doesn't it?

Another tiger—an escaped one—made a short but lively trip through the town on 28 January.

Escaping from a cage in Rochor Road, he started off on his self-conducted tour of Singapore. Trotting up Rochor Road he turned into Victoria Street and then into Bencoolen Street, the people in the streets flying shrieking before him, while ignorant Indians were rushing about the town spreading the news that they had seen the devil!

Coming to a vacant plot in Bencoolen Street the tiger, who was quite as much afraid of the populace as they were of him, crept inside the fence and laid down for a rest.

Meanwhile Singapore was arming! The first *shikari* to come on the field was Private Ariana of the SVI, armed with his trusty rifle. Accompanying him was his brother, with a twelve-bore double-barrelled gun, loaded with ball. This vanguard of the subsequent army of hunters stalked Stripes to his empty plot and opened fire.

Private Ariana's first shot hit one end of the tiger! Some said it was the end where the head was, some said the other. At all events the tiger was very annoyed, and with a roar jumped up and sprang out of sight. He cleared a six-foot wall, and as he jumped brother Ariana put two twelve-bore bullets into his body.

With a roar of anguish the tiger dashed down Brunei Lane, scattering the morning crowd like sparks from a rocket. The screams of the frightened populace vied with the roars of the tiger, and chaos ensued.

At the upper end of the lane stood a house, with its dark door invitingly open. The house was full of coolies, jabbering at their work so loudly that they had not attempted even to listen to the noise outside. Into that open doorway sprang the tiger. Whether he hurt any of the Chinese is not known, for they were never seen again! And under a bunk the tiger came to rest.

Meanwhile, as I have said, Singapore had been arming, and soon a crowd of all kinds, armed with shotguns and crackers, were besieging the house and throwing crackers in an endeavour to draw the tiger. When he refused to come out, even after crackers had been thrown through the windows, the armed force began firing slugs and buckshot into him.

They were still firing volleys when a European inspector and a Sikh corporal appeared on the scene, armed with Snyders and more buckshot, and these two officially killed the tiger. It was then legally pronounced dead and its body was drawn from its hiding place. That is to say, an attempt was made to do so, but it is alleged that there was not enough whole skin left on the carcass to hold it properly together. However, the remains were bundled into a cart and the funeral procession formed. The remains of the tiger were duly returned to the safe custody of its sorrowing owner in Rochor Road.

And then the fun began. A Mr Lim Chin Hin claimed to be the hero of the day, a claim which was stoutly repudiated in a letter to the press by the Ariana brothers, who offered to produce over a hundred witnesses. To this letter Lim Chin Hin replied. He offered S$1 per head to a charity to be named by the paper for every witness produced up to one hundred, and asked why, if the Arianas mortally wounded the tiger, as they claimed to have done, did they beat such a precipitable retreat after firing?

Another gentleman, signing himself 'a lover of bravery', wrote that merit should not go unrewarded, and suggested medals for Messrs Ariana, Lim Chin Hin and a certain Akbar, who also seemed to have had an outside claim, the particulars of which I cannot discover.

However, like all other excitements the matter was soon forgotten when other and more important matters attracted public attention.

And the next happening was enough to drive all thoughts

of tigers and small matters like that out of our minds, for Japan declared war on Russia! That is to say, Japan assumed the initiative in a situation that had become so hopeless that the respective embassies were withdrawn. This occurred on Monday, 8 February and, of course, the news filled the papers to the exclusion of everything else.

It is not my intention, however, to do more than note the matter; this is a personal diary of local happenings, not a history of the world.

I started playing football again this year, and was back in the field as goalkeeper for the club. We were supposed to have a very strong team, and it certainly gave a good account of itself this season. It is, of course, difficult to judge the merits of football after a lapse of thirty years or so, but I feel that Singapore seldom sees in the field today individual football players of the merit of Teddy Bradbery, Ellerton, Ker, Dick and Farrer, to mention a few. Perhaps, however, I am prejudiced.

An attempt was made early this year to restart the choral branch of the Philharmonic Society, which had languished and died after Major St Clair's cutting remarks reported in a previous chapter.

Several of these resuscitations were attempted, but they never came to anything much. Choral singing, except in opera, never held up its head again until many years later, when the present musical society came into being at the opening of the St Clair organ in 1931.

A big steamer fire occurred in the harbour on 1 March. The

SS *Glenturret* caught fire at the wharfs. She was full of copra, and the outbreak soon became so serious that it was decided to tow her clear of the wharf and anchor her in the roads. Various methods were tried to get the fire under control, but all were unavailing, and at noon the question of scuttling the ship was seriously discussed. However, by two o'clock next morning the fire was under control, the ship being, by this time, waterlogged.

It was one of the biggest shipping fires that Singapore had ever seen, and as the anchorage of the burning vessel was off Fort Palmer, everyone had a good view of the disaster.

A certain Madame Blanche Arral, an operatic singer of great merit, passed through Singapore about this time. Though she did not sign in public, she gave two concerts, one at the Teutonia Club and the other at the Tanglin Club. At the latter concert Mrs Salzmann and I assisted her. It is of this occasion that I have written elsewhere, commenting on the quiet beauty of Mrs Salzmann's singing of 'The Old Grey Mare' in contradistinction to the coloratura efforts of Madame Arral.

It will interest some of the present-day agitators for municipal franchise to hear how nobly [*sic*] electors responded to the demands made upon their votes thirty and more years ago. For strange as it may appear, municipal commissioners were still being elected for the various wards into which Singapore was divided as late as 1904. In that year, Mr C.B. Buckley stood for Kallang Ward, and in the absence of any competitor was duly nominated. But he still had to be elected, and required the large amount of twenty-one votes before he could take possession of his seat. Could he get them? No, he couldn't. Buckley could do most things but he couldn't make the citizens of Singapore turn up at the municipal offices to record a vote. But then neither could other people! For the Tanjong Pagar Ward had just previously been given three chances to poll twenty-one votes for their own candidate, and failed every time! In fact it was always a matter of wonder how would-be commissioners ever managed to find anyone to nominate them!

It used to be the habit of the governor, after such farces as those mentioned above, to step in, exercise his prerogative and 'appoint' the non-elected nominee to the vacant seat.

In March 1904 the first move was made to start a country club in Singapore. It is interesting to remember this because, from time to time afterwards, the same agitation was to be started, taken a certain distance and then dropped.

The arguments for the club seemed to be the same every time. Here they are set out in the agitation of 1904:

> 1. What is there in Singapore for anyone to do on a wet afternoon after business if one is not a member of the Singapore Club?
> 2. There is nowhere to go after dinner except to the hotels or bed.
> 3. The SCC closes every afternoon at seven o'clock in the evening and has no attractions except the playing fields and the bar.
> 4. The Ladies' Lawn pavilion space is so abbreviated

that it is hardly large enough to shelter playing members from a shower of rain.

5. The Tanglin Club is hopeless. It has been declared dangerous and, in any case, is only used—with the exception of the bowling alley—for an occasional evening dance etc., etc.

These complaints were, as a matter of fact, perfectly true, and they were not only true of 1904 but of many years to come.

The Teutonia Club was pointed to as a model of what was wanted, and it certainly was a flourishing club with amenities. Food could be obtained there, there were a few living rooms and dances, concerts, dramatic performances, etc. were frequent. Tennis, skittles, billiards, cards and other indoor games were also provided.

As I have said, these agitations cropped up from time to time and came to nothing. The one that most nearly succeeded was the project, some years later, when private motorcars were coming into fashion. This project had as its foundation the lease of Tyersall. This scheme was all cut and dried, and I believe the option on the property had been obtained. But for some reason which I never discovered it also fell through just when it looked like coming into being.

I am always sorry that it did not eventuate. It would have combined all the amenities of the present Tanglin Club with the Ladies' Lawn and the Polo Club, and even a golf course was proposed for the grounds. Roland Braddell was at the back of the scheme, and I know that it was a great disappointment to him that it failed.

There had now arrived in Singapore a certain Lieutenant Abbott and wife. The lady was a distinct acquisition to Singapore, both in musical and dramatic circles. She was vivacious, pretty and *petite*, possessed a charming voice and with acting ability above the ordinary. She had, I believe, been playing lead in one of George Edwardes' travelling companies before her marriage. From the moment of her first appearance at a Philharmonic concert in March, she loomed large in all entertainments of a lighter nature that took place. She helped considerably to add to the gaiety of life while her husband was stationed here.

The SVR was still lingering on. It appeared in corps orders for the first time that year on 13 March, with an intimation that there would be field firing at Pasir Panjang. I suppose that, having failed to get rid of the die-hards already referred to, they were making the best of a bad job and waiting, like Mr Micawber, for something to turn up.

But no, it was not to be. For no one turned up to this field-firing parade, and a few days later there appeared in the papers, within a deep border of black, the obituary notice:

THE SINGAPORE VOLUNTEER RIFLES

DEEPLY REGRETTED

His Excellency the Governor had exercised the powers vested in him, and had directed that the SVR should be discontinued as a separate unit.

But he gave us another chance. 'His Excellency the Governor'—the notice went on to say—'has been pleased to authorise the formation of a Maxim Section in the corps in lieu of the SVR.'

A few days later a meeting was held at the drill hall at which all the die-hards, numbering about thirty, were present. The unit was formed with four subsections which were to be presided over by Sergeants J.G. Mactaggart, D.Y. Perkins, J.A.S. Jennings and B. Berry.

We all signed on and the Maxim Company, SVC, a unit which has had a long and enthusiastic career, was born. It is continued today in the shape of the Machine Gun Company, SVC, a unit of the new corps which is exceedingly smart and *very* proud of itself, as it has every reason to be.

More about the growing pains of the new unit later on.

I must refer here to one of the most remarkable performances I have ever witnessed on the stage of the Singapore theatre. The Zancigs, Mr and Mrs, passed through Singapore. These people were to create a furore later on in London; I saw them here before they had made their name. They called themselves The Mysterious Zancigs, and their show was thought-provoking.

Mary and Edie Abrams, Bill Sykes, Criswick and myself decided to go and see them, so we made up a party and went to the cheap seats at the back of the hall for fun. Mrs Zancig was seated on the stage, blindfolded, and 'hubby' wandered about the audience asking people in a low voice what they wanted his wife to do, and she did it! In due course he came to us, and just as he reached our line of seats I notice Daddy Abrams come in and take his accustomed seat at the end of the front row. I had a brainwave. I whispered to Zancig that I wanted his wife to go to the old gentleman who had just come in, get a dollar out of his trouser pocket and bring it to me. (It must be remembered that Daddy didn't know we were there.)

Nothing happened, as far as I could see. Zancig remained standing quietly beside me, when all of a sudden his wife got up from her chair and, blindfolded as she was, commenced to feel her way to the side of the stage where there was a platform leading into the auditorium. Down this she came and went straight to the seat where Daddy was sitting, much to his surprise. But surprise changed to alarm when she grabbed his arm, made him stand up and began to fumble for his trouser pockets!

By this time the audience were roaring with laughter, and hadn't the remotest knowledge of the reason for all this fun, for no one but those in our little party had heard my wish expressed. Madame Zancig got that dollar, brought it right down the centre of the hall to me and dropped it in my hand.

How the thing was done, except through the medium of real telepathy, I cannot imagine.

I stood Daddy a drink at the Europe afterwards with his own money, but from that day to this I have wondered what would have happened if Daddy had not had a dollar in his pocket!

To revert to the formation of the Maxim Company. The first trouble arose over the guns themselves. The SVA, headed in their arguments by their gallant major, St Clair, maintained that the guns belonged to them (they had in fact been presented to them by a private donor). Therefore any personnel that manned them must be of the SVA and wear their uniform. The men who enlisted in the Maxim Company, however, were men who had *refused* to join the SVA at the disbanding of the SVR. So their argument was that as the SVA couldn't man the Maxims themselves they could not, in fairness, refuse to let them be manned by the Maxim Company.

But though this argument sounded logical it did not suit the gunners, and St Clair, in his capacity of OC, SVA, even threatened to take the guns away altogether.

What actual legal and documentary rights he held in support of this threat I never discovered. In the end a compromise was effected whereby we wore the SVA badge on our shoulders with a small 'M' in brackets tacked on, and also the famous blue puttees of the gunners. Those blue puttees, by the way, were the finest things ever issued to the Volunteers. I have mine yet, in almost as good a condition as when they were issued. They were straight and not shaped to the leg, and also much longer than modern puttees to allow for the numerous twists that had to be given to them when putting them on. I use mine now, as we used our spare ones then, to put round my body like a cummerbund when I have, or have a chance of getting, a chill.

Then another difficulty cropped up. In order to get the company up to strength the sergeants went round the town recruiting. They took the names of everyone who was willing to support the effort, whether they had any intention of putting in drills or not. All that was necessary was that they should be able to pay the S$25 fine for inefficiency when called upon to do so! Consequently the paper strength of the company was good, but the number of workers comparatively small. When, later on, I was made a sergeant in charge of a section, I had to clear out at least fifty percent of the people who were supposed to be in my charge, for they never turned up to drill and never had had any intention of doing so.

However, in spite of these growing pains the company thrived and, guided by such well-known Volunteers as Tongue, Lobb, Hay, etc., the sections soon reached a stage of efficiency when they could begin to take a pride in themselves. And that efficiency has continued undimmed to the present day. I take my hat off to the Machine Gun Company of today, which, under its popular leader, Captain Goldman, is nobly carrying on the traditions that were born in the early months of 1904.

For the benefit of the visiting cricketers from upcountry at Easter, Billy Dunman, Mrs Abbott and myself produced *The Rose of Auvergne*, a delightful operetta by Offenbach.

It deals with the loves of a blacksmith and a cobbler for the prepossessing proprietress of the village inn. Billy was the cobbler and I was the blacksmith. In the story the cobbler is the successful suitor, and in revenge the blacksmith comes and smashes up the happy home.

We had a big old-fashioned dresser made, which we hung with old pottery ware collected from the multitudinous samples in the hands of the firms. Each night I used to smash the lot, then go round next day and collect more from the various godowns.

Now, as I have said, the front seats of the audience were very near the footlights, and the stage was very low. One night Sir William Taylor, the acting governor, and his sister came to the show and, as usual, had the seats of honour in the front row. When the pottery-smashing time came I noticed that the party from Government House got up and left.

Next day we found out that a piece of broken pottery had jumped the footlights and fallen at Miss Taylor's feet. The party had thereupon left because, as they averred later, Mr Dunman and Mr Brown were very much the worse for liquor. Mr Brown so much so, indeed, that he had taken to smashing the furniture on the stage!

My representation of an angry blacksmith had evidently been too realistic!

Sir John Anderson, the new governor of the colony, arrived in Singapore on Saturday, 16 April of this year. The usual ceremonial customary on the arrival of such an important personage was gone through. The ladies of the town wore their best frocks, and the seniors and officials among the men wore their frock coats and top hats. It was said that on these occasions it was possible to judge the length of time a man had been in the colony from the greenness of his frock coat and the shape of this topper! At weddings and suchlike functions it was quite possible for bridegroom and best man to borrow a fairly new-looking outfit. However, on occasions such as the arrival of a governor everyone had to wear his own, for all the others were in use!

It has been said that one of the most interesting sartorial sights that Singapore has ever seen was the funeral of a former governor, Sir Charles Mitchell, who was a prominent mason. The whole of that celebrated fraternity turned up in full regalia and evening dress, in the sunlight. The clothes showed many shades of colour, but *none were black*!

The bachelors of the town used to hold balls in these old days. One such was held at the end of April in the town hall, and Sir John Anderson and his daughter made their first appearance in public at it. These functions were very select, and ladies who received invitations used to look down their noses at their unfortunate sisters who were left out in the cold. I suspect that the bachelors' committee that arranged the invitation list were not envied very much by their fellows!

The real [*sic*] sea serpent was seen by a full ship's crew off the coast of Cochin–China at the end of May. The French gunboat *Decidée* was cruising in the bay of Halong, near Haiphong, when about 300 yards from the vessel a black mass was observed, which was taken at first for a rock. Later on the supposed rock moved, and it was then thought to be a colossal turtle. Shortly afterwards, however, the mass stretched out in vertical undulations and what appeared to be a flattened serpent, about a hundred feet long, became plainly visible. The serpent dived twice before the eyes of all on board. Once, it went right under the gunboat and came up on the other side so near that those on board were able, by leaning over the gunwale, to get a good view of the monster. It was seen that the head and neck were turtle-like, and the skin was dark brown with rings of patches of yellow. The animal emitted jets of vapoury water, and afterwards disappeared in the distance. I give this information for what it is worth. One may believe it or not, as one chooses.

Early in June the amateurs were busy again, producing a play called *The Duchess of Bayswater* along with a repetition of *The Rose of Auvergne*. I produced the two items on the programme and played again in the latter piece. *The Duchess of Bayswater* was not a very good choice, but it had the merit of producing a good laugh, which is what audiences of those days liked, just as they do today. Bill Sykes, already famous for his performance in the *Yeomen*, played the character lead and was excellent. The next important male part was in the hands of Tommy Treadgold, still a resident here and at that time on the staff of the Hong Kong and Shanghai Bank. Mrs Mayson (then Miss Newton) and Mrs Hooper had the principal female parts.

It was about this time that the Chinese in Malaya began to discard their *towchang*—or, to use a more popular word for the Westerner, their queues. The Selangor Literary Society, a Chinese association, held a full-dress debate upon the matter, and as a result several well-known Chinese gentlemen appeared in public with their hair cut. The movement had really started as far back as 1898, but had met with considerable opposition. It was not until the revolution in China, however, that the habit became general, though among the more enlightened members of the Straits-born Chinese community, it really commenced in earnest in this year 1904.

HMS *Cadmus*, afterwards to become famous during the mutiny in 1915, passed through Singapore on her way to the Australian station in June. She had been commissioned at Sheerness on 13 April.

At the annual sports of the SCC this year, I took away another mug for five-a-side football, playing in a team that included Darbyshire and that was captained by Bradbery. These five-a-side games were great fun. There were very many entries, so the tournament kept those who were the winners very busy in the evenings, and we got lots of strenuous exercise.

11

The YMCA had been officially started in 1903. In July 1904 the first annual general meeting was held at Zetland House, which had been taken by the association as their headquarters. The Whitefields had moved their boarding house into the more residential district of Singapore, and Armenian Street and Orchard Road as far as the railway bridge—which was now built—were rapidly becoming business thoroughfares. However, for some years to come private houses remained sandwiched in among the shops.

One of the first moves made by Sir John Anderson after his appointment as governor was to ask the Legislative Council to assent to the expenditure of a large sum of money on the Singapore harbour. The Tanjong Pagar Dock Company was still a private concern, and there was big discussion in the council as to the advisability of the expenditure. In the end, though, the first reading of the bill was carried unanimously. Here, then, is the real beginning of a movement which was to end with the Tanjong Pagar Dock Company being taken over by the government, and the whole of the docks and harbour coming under the control of the colony.

A wonderful mirage was noticed in the Singapore harbour on 4 July. Away on the horizon was seen a fully rigged ship, and those looking at it were astonished to see that the vessel—masts, sails and spars all complete—was reflected hanging in the sky. One vessel was right way up, the other was upside down. The mirage slowly disappeared as the ship sailed out of sight. A most unusual phenomenon for this part of the world.

Proposals were put forward in July for the rebuilding of the Hotel de l'Europe, with Messrs Swan & McLaren as the architects. At this time, as I have already written, the Europe was a long low building consisting of a ground floor and one other storey. It extended from the corner of High Street along what is now known as St Andrew's Road, and merged into the municipal offices. The new plans were for a three-storied building, with lifts and electric lighting, a tremendous move towards modernisation. The hotel was to go through various vicissitudes before it was finally erected. Today as I write (1934), the last of that then wonderful building is disappearing under the crowbars of the housebreakers to make room for a row of flats. The outside wall on St Andrew's Road will be about the only part of the old building that will be left.

On 6 July in Sarawak, the wife of Bishop Hose, bishop of Sarawak and Singapore, passed to her last rest. She was a dear lady and I knew her, her husband and children very well indeed. Her death was a great blow to the bishop, and to a host of people in these parts who knew and loved her. The reredos in St Andrew's Cathedral was later erected in her memory.

And now began the trouble concerning the pulling down of the old town hall. It was a move which was to bring disaster to musical activity in Singapore, and to undo all the wonderful work that Salzmann and St Clair had done to make Singapore a musically minded city.

On 10 August the papers came out with leaders on the subject. The substance of their complaint was that it had been understood, if not definitely promised, that no alteration to the old town hall should be attempted until the new Memorial Hall had been completed and had been proven to be an acoustic success. The matter was so important at the time—and history has proved that it was even more vital than was anticipated then—that it will be well to discourse on the happenings at some length.

As I have already mentioned, the European element had voted for a new theatre as a memorial to the late Queen Victoria. The governor, Sir Frank Swettenham, had very wisely vetoed that proposal on the grounds that the native element in the place would probably not subscribe to a building that would be of use to only a small portion of the community. So a public hall was eventually decided upon. This public hall—to be called the Victoria Memorial Hall—was now in the course of erection, but it was not expected to be ready for use for another twelve to eighteen months.

The proposal, therefore, to start the demolition of the old hall at this time was foolish in the extreme. The reasons against the move were set out in leaded type by *The Straits Times* in a very forcible leader. It will be well to repeat those reasons here, because time was to prove them to be only too true.

1. There will be no covered meeting place in the town
for a period of eighteen months to two years.

2. The Philharmonic Society's concerts and reunions, as
well as all musical entertainments, will be absolutely
stopped.

3. The annual and historic Christmas entertainments,
at which 700 to 800 children are amused, will
be absolutely stopped.

4. The travelling theatrical companies, who make their
living by acting, will be turned away from the town.

5. All public dances and entertainments will be stopped.

These were the five principal reasons given, and there were
many others. All were founded on the experience of men who
were actually engaged in the entertainment of Singapore, and who
really knew what they were talking about, but who had not been
consulted.

One of these reasons was against the building of the theatre
next to the Memorial Hall. It was pointed out that if this were
done the two places could never be used simultaneously, and it
would be impossible to remedy the error once it had been made.
(The error *was* made, the prophecy has turned out to be only too
true and the only remedy is now to scrap one of the buildings
entirely and erect it somewhere else.)

Of the five reasons given by *The Straits Times*, the only one
that did not turn out to be absolutely correct was the one about
the Philharmonic concerts. Through the courtesy of the Germans,

their club was put at the society's disposal for concerts while the demolition of the old hall was going on. However, the absence of a place to store musical instruments, of a hall for regular practice and of a general meeting place for the members, was keenly felt.

But I think that the greatest of all the disasters that were to come with the pulling down of the old town hall, was the destruction of one of the most perfect rooms, acoustically, that it has ever been my lot to sing in or to listen to music in. It really *was* perfect, and I am certain that there were no halls in the East like it. It was not big, but it was big enough to have lasted Singapore for another ten years or so as a public hall, and would have been exceedingly useful today for small meetings and concerts of chamber music. Singapore would have been very well advised if it had kept that old town hall standing as there would have been ample use for it today.

Well, the ball had now started rolling and it rolled along swiftly. Frizell, the manager of Chartered Bank and chairman of the Memorial Committee, wrote a long letter of over a column to *The Straits Times*. Buckley and Salzmann followed with letters just as long. St Clair in his paper, the *Singapore Free Press*, commenced his campaign against the vandalism of the government which he never retired from until he left Singapore for good. The whole town was unanimous that the words of the people mentioned above were the words of people who knew what they were talking about, and that further advice should be taken by the committee before any further move was made in the matter. Sadly all that was promised was, in the words of Frizell's letter, that 'The committee would be willing to receive advice.' It is not recorded, however, that they were prepared to go out and ask for it. They seemed certain—knowing nothing whatever of the subject—that because Mr Bidwell, the architect, had been for three years an assistant to the architect of the London County Council in respect of London theatres, he could guarantee to build a hall the acoustic properties of which would be good. They were, of course, never more mistaken in their lives. They produced eventually, in the Memorial Hall, a building which, from an acoustic standpoint, was absolutely impossible. It was entirely useless from the vocal or instrumental point of view, it defeated the efforts of every speaker and its erection, and the simultaneous destruction of the old town hall, sounded the death knell for music in Singapore. This is no exaggeration, but an absolute historical fact. Music had no home, no place where it could be cultivated and listened to, and it died.

For over twenty years Singapore was to suffer because of the refusal of that Memorial Committee to listen to the advice of those who knew what they were talking about. And not only that. Their action in killing the musical spirit in the place made it most extraordinarily difficult for the few who remained faithful to revive the art when the time came. The local-born children of 1904 grew up to manhood without any knowledge of what music could do for them and their lives. Instead of being musically conscious, as St Clair used to dream they would be, when they reached manhood they knew nothing about the art. The great work of St Clair and Salzmann, built up with such care, trouble and enthusiasm, had to be started all over again by another generation.

Looking back upon the matter after all these years I am able to see clearly facts which, at that time, could only be assumed. It is possible to say now that St Clair, Salzmann and Co. were entirely right, and the Memorial Committee entirely wrong.

Well, the argument went on. The papers wrote long leaders and printed long letters, but all to no purpose. In due course the demolition of the old hall began. I shall have more to say upon this subject from time to time, for the erection and existence of these two buildings entered largely into the activities of my life in Singapore.

The Tanglin Club had, for some time, been rather a white elephant. The building was old and rather dismal-looking, and had indeed been condemned as unsafe. From this time onwards various schemes were put forward by authoritative committees and private individuals for bringing the club up to date, or for altering it altogether.

The first of these schemes was put forward in August 1904 by a committee appointed to report upon the matter.

This committee suggested the removal of the club to the corner of Orchard Road and Orange Grove Road (land, I believe, owned by 'Honest John' Anderson of Guthrie & Co.). The scheme was to cost about S$300,000, and was to include the land, a new building with residential quarters for men, tennis courts, stables, bowling alleys and all the other necessities of an up-to-date social club of that day.

The scheme—like every other scheme to move the club—fell through, and the Tanglin Club today is on the same site that it occupied since its birth. Indeed it consists very largely of the original building that we condemned over thirty years ago!

It will be necessary to refer again to the question of the town hall because of the all-important meeting that was held on 9 September. It was a meeting that was presided over by His Excellency, the governor, and at which all the leading men of Singapore at that time were present. The calling of this meeting had been forced upon the Memorial Committee by the strength of the attack against their proposals to pull down the old town hall and convert it into a theatre.

Now, it must be remembered that this decision was come to by the committee just two years back and, as I have already mentioned in these pages, the proposed plans for the alterations had been published in the papers.

There had been no opposition to the suggestions at the time. No doubt this was because the whole matter was very much in the future then, the building of the Memorial Hall having hardly started.

But when the suggestion was made to begin pulling down the old hall before the new one was ready, the growing dissatisfaction against the original scheme crystallised and resulted in the very definite expressions of disapproval that I have referred to.

Hence this very important meeting—at which the governor, Mr Frizell, Hon. G.S. Murray, Mr Buckley, Major St Clair and others all spoke, and at length.

Mr Buckley wanted to move a definite resolution that no portion of the subscriptions to the Victoria Memorial should be used to convert the old town hall into a theatre. The governor, possibly not knowing his Buckley then as well as he was to know him later, ruled him out of order because notice of motion had not been given. Buckley, however, remarked that the meeting had been quite ready to listen to the governor, and that they could now listen to the other side of the argument. He proceeded to read his motion and to speak at length upon it. And what he said was very much to the point, and most of his prognostications have turned out to be true! One point he made was that the Supreme Court would be disturbed by the noise of rehearsals! Why they hadn't been disturbed till then by rehearsals in the old town hall, I never found out, but it is a curious fact that on several occasions since they have made complaints. Only the other day (1934) someone in the Memorial Hall had to stop playing the organ at the request of the judge in court across the way! Is the spirit of old Buckley hovering round, endeavouring to prove that what he said at that meeting of long ago was correct?

Major St Clair was told that his arguments were stultified by the fact that he had, in his paper, agreed originally to the scheme. The fact that he had found that he had been wrong and admitted it, instead of being recognised as the result of careful study of the matter, was held to be proof that his opinions were of no account!

The Straits Times, in a leader dealing with the meeting, was very caustic. Starting with the sentence:

'One of the most objectionable features of all administrative measures in the Straits—be they official or merely communal—is the fact that it is considered bad form to acknowledge an error.'

The paper went on to say, with reference to Mr Buckley's motion:

'The fact that the resolution was denied consideration by the Chair tended to render obscure the purpose for which the general meeting had been called. With the exception of Mr Buckley's remarks and the statement in self-defence elicited from Mr St Clair, the majority of the time of the meeting was occupied in listening to denunciations of those persons who have had the temerity to hold views alien to those of the Committee. Those rashly minded gentlemen departed from the meeting under the impression that they were welcome to call a meeting on their own account if they wanted to, but that it did not matter much whether they did or not.'

And the leader finishes up as follows:

'We may reiterate the fact that practically the entire musical world of Singapore holds views on the subject similar to those expressed by Mr Buckley.'

And *The Straits Times* was correct—we did, and time has proved that we were right. Every single one of the disadvantages that were pointed out at the time have been proved up to the hilt to be true, with the possible exception of the one about the danger to the Memorial Hall if fire broke out in the theatre. And let us hope that that remains for ever an unprovable statement.

Here is a little paragraph from the papers of September that will interest the rubber industry of today.

'A consignment of Seremban rubber biscuits was sold in Colombo a fortnight ago. Mr R.B. Creasy procured the parcel, after competition, at R3.75 per pound ... There is no doubt that any good lots of rubber will find a ready sale in the English markets in London and Liverpool, or on the continent.'

Rather humorous to read today, isn't it? And even more so to note that America isn't even mentioned!

I have been informed by a friend who has read this manuscript that the actual sample of that first consignment of Singapore rubber is still to be seen in a certain office in Colombo.

On 17 October Miss St Clair, the daughter of Major St Clair, was married to Lieutenant Buchan of the Manchesters.

Reading of this wedding brings to my mind many jolly mornings spent with Miss St Clair, Mary Abrams, Buchan, Sykes, Bolingbroke and others, enjoying a sport which has, to a very large extent, disappeared from the place, to wit: riding. In those old days Sunday morning riding parties were the rule rather than the exception, and indeed those who followed the sport used to ride regularly during the week before going to the office. Many kept their own horses, and those who did not could hire excellent mounts from Dallans or Abrams. The horses used to be sent up to one's house and one could ride almost anywhere, for there were no macadam roads in those days, and the soft laterite was excellent and easy for the horses. Kathé St Clair was an exceedingly nice girl with no nonsense about her, an excellent rider and a real good pal, and our little party had many delightful rides together.

When she married the cathedral was crowded with friends and well-wishers. We gave her a fully choral wedding, a thing which was then, as it is now, a gesture of respect and friendship from the cathedral choir.

Talking about riding reminds me of one or two stories that should not be forgotten. There was, for instance, the man—I won't mention names—who was in the habit of drinking rather heavily at night. After dinner he would get into his riding breeches and top-boots, then proceed with his usual potations, falling at last into bed just as he was. In the morning his boy would wake him, he would get up and onto his horse and ride off the effects of the night's debauch. I suppose the idea was that he would have been totally unable to stoop down to put his boots on in the morning, so he did it the night before!

One night, about one o'clock in the morning, I was awakened by a horse galloping madly around the garden underneath my bedroom window. I woke up and so did my messmates. Now McMillan was driving—and riding—an ex-racehorse named Deadlight, rather a fiery creature and very fast. Mrs Waddell, who lived in the big house above us and whose garden adjoined ours, also rode regularly and, of course, kept her own horse. As we leant out of our windows to try and see what was happening we heard a lady's voice calling into the darkness: '*Siapa punya kuda? Siapa punya kuda?*'

Immediately followed the gruff voice of Wullie Waddell: 'Awa' tae your bed, wumman, it's no' your horse, it's McMullan's!'

How we did laugh! As a matter of fact it was Mrs Waddell's

pony after all!

Sunday morning rides used to be long affairs. A start would be made, say at six o'clock, joining up with others by previous arrangement. Away the cavalcade would go, sometimes ten, sometimes twenty strong, returning about nine o'clock. Sometimes it was even as late as ten o'clock or after if, as often happened, a halt had been made at a halfway house for slings and other liquid refreshment. Very often, on our return, we would all finish at the house of one of the party where our boys would be with a change of clothes. After a bath we would sit down to a tremendous breakfast—tiffin of curry—and get home about noon or one o'clock and go straight to bed. Two meals a day was the rule on Sundays, and a very good rule it was, too.

The amateurs were in harness again for the October races, and produced a variety show, and a farce called *Aunt Charlotte's Maid*. The cast of this farce was a particularly strong one and included Mrs Hooper, Miss Newton (now Mrs Mayson), Mrs Abbott, Sykes, Abbott and a Lieutenant Davidson, RA, one of the very finest comedians Singapore has ever had among its amateurs. I produced, and we scored a tremendous success. The first part of the programme consisted of musical items. The versatility of the cast is shown by the fact that the Abbotts, Sykes, Maudie Mayson, Davidson and myself all contributed songs and duets. Sykes and Dunman were again to the fore with their 'Cock and Bull' duet from the *Yeomen*, and also with their topical verses, which were vociferously encored. At each recall they seemed to be ready with another verse. Races, opium farms, Harbour Board schemes—they had skits on them all. A great evening!

Unfortunately, owing to bereavement in the family of one of the cast, we were unable to repeat the performance as had been intended.

It is worth while noting here that the Harbour Improvement Scheme was being fiercely debated about this time. It is not my intention to do more in this narrative than just mention the fact. Other and better writers than I have dealt with the matter in full on various occasions. But it was, of course, a matter of general discussion in the clubs, messes and business circles. As such I refer to it; and leave it at that.

Sir John Anderson, with his daughter as hostess, gave his first King's birthday ball at Government House on 9 November. Government House balls, in those days, were much more colourful than they are today. Mess uniform was not worn. Review Order was the rule, and red coats and gold lace were very conspicuous. All officers wore swords and carried their helmets on their arm. It was not until after the reception—which was held in the drawing room upstairs and was a lengthy affair, everyone being received— that these articles of full dress was discarded. The retrieving of the right sword after the ball was over was sometimes a difficult matter! On this particular occasion the dancing was made much more comfortable than before by the fact that electric fans had been installed in the ballroom, but even then the crowd was tremendous. Government House had not then been enlarged. Sir John Anderson and his daughter were excellent at entertaining people, and a night at Government House, either official or unofficial, was always a very pleasant function. In the days to come I was to get to know them both very well indeed, and their kindness, hospitality and absence of side in their own home will always be remembered by me as ideal.

It may interest those with a military penchant to know that at the parade that morning of the garrison troops, the Malay Submarine Diving Section of the RE were present. I think this was probably the last time they appeared on a King's birthday parade as they were disbanded some time after. I believe their first officer was a certain Lieutenant Ridout, afterwards Major-General Ridout, in charge of the Singapore defences during the war.

The Philharmonic Orchestra was still going strong, and gave a show on 26 November in the Teutonia Club which was kindly placed at their disposal by the Germans. This concert was a great success, the orchestra being strengthened by several men from the string band of HMS *Cressy*, a battleship in port at the time. This was the last concert which the wind players from the band of the Manchester Regiment attended, the battalion going to India shortly afterwards. I sang the prologue to *Pagliacci* at this concert, and also took part in a trio from *Princess Ida*, singing the tenor part with Sykes and Criswick of that lovely number 'They intend to send a wire to the moon'.

On Saturday, 3 December the chorus (resuscitated again) and the orchestra gave a performance in the town hall of Cowan's *Rose Maiden*. Mrs Krarup, Maudie Newton, Mrs Hooper, Cunradi and myself were the soloists. Whitefield was conducting during the absence of Major St Clair who was on leave, and altogether it was said to have been an excellent show.

On 13 December the Manchester Regiment marched out of Tanglin Barracks on their way to India, and the 1st Battalion of the Notts and Derby Regiment (the Sherwood Foresters) marched in. They were commanded by a certain Lieutenant-Colonel Watts, about whom I have written in 'The Bad Old Days'. It was said of him that he had such a liver that his officers dare not join the Garrison Golf Club for fear he would ask them to play with him! The liver was there all right; I've seen it in action but I cannot vouch for the remainder of the story!

The discussions about the harbour scheme that had been going on for some time, and the comments by public and private individuals concerning the working of the Tanjong Pagar Dock Company, were brought to a head on Tuesday, 20 December. A cable from London said that the directors of the dock company had been formally notified by the Secretary of State for the Colonies that the government intended to expropriate the property of the company. To many people, even to those high in the service of the dock company, the news seemed to be literally a bolt from the blue. It was certainly the most important local happening that had taken place in the colony for very many years.

That it was a good move was the general opinion because it was recognised on all sides that the company was rather out of date. A very large sum would be required to carry out the rehabilitation and modernising of the property which was very necessary and, in fact, overdue.

However, lots of things had to be done before the transfer could take place. As the whole history of the matter is admirably set forth in the colony's centenary publication, *One Hundred Years of Singapore*, there is no need to do more here than mention the date of the actual decision to transfer.

For some time now there had been rumours of mysterious happenings at Fort Canning where the Hong Kong and Singapore Battery of the Royal Garrison Artillery, with their officers, were in residence. It was said that most of the officers had given up soldiering and had taken to other pursuits. It was also said that ladies and gentlemen having no connection with the military were frequently coming and going from the fort, and at night, too. There was a good deal of speculation as to what was going on.

The secret was well kept, however. It was not until the guests received their invitations to be present at a 'Grand performance of the pantomime *Cinderella*' that the truth came out.

The idea emanated from one of the subalterns of the battery, a Lieutenant Biggs. He offered to write the pantomime if the others would do the rest. I was consulted with the result that 'the rest'— which consisted merely of reconditioning a building honoured by the name of the theatre, designing, making and painting the scenery and all properties, procuring the costumes, etc.—was accepted, and Biggs was told to get on with the good work.

I have very pleasant memories of those months spent at Fort Canning. A bedroom in the old mess was placed at my disposal, and I spent most of my nights there. I would go up to the fort straight from the office, get into my oldest clothes and with my assistants—they comprised most of the other officers—would set to work. I was appointed the general consent foreman of works, and great fun it was. We would slave away with our tools and paint brushes until about half past seven in the evening, then have a bath and change, dine on the veranda and be ready for the others, who would come up at nine o'clock for a rehearsal. Our real ladies—there were synthetic ones in the show also—were Mrs Abbott, Miss Newton and Miss Edie Newton (now Mrs Griffith Jones). Whitefield looked after the musical work for us. The rest of the workers and performers were all subalterns, and included some of the best talent that Singapore has ever had. Davidson and Pope were both exceedingly clever comedians, and Watson and Biggs were also good.

The major in charge of the battery was named Burton, affectionately called Piggy. He had had, I believe, a lot to do with the using of caterpillar-wheeled steam engines in the Boer War, and he owned one of the first motor bicycles that ever appeared in Singapore. He used to spend his Sunday mornings taking his bike to pieces under the old mess house, and the afternoons in putting it together again. He was very hospitable but, alas, very forgetful. If he were introduced to anyone in the club he would say: 'God bless you, come and dine with us at the mess next Thursday.' It was a regular formula with him, and caused us a lot of trouble during our preparations for the pantomime. For on Thursdays, the regular mess night, congratulating ourselves that no one was coming to dinner, we would get into tennis shirts for our veranda meal. As often as not a gharry would drive into the porch and deposit a splendidly arrayed gentleman, tail coat and white tie all complete, who would walk in and ask for Major Burton. With a groan one of the subs would have to rush off, change into mess kit and dine in solemn state with the visitor, while Burton, who had invited him, would probably be fast asleep and comfortable in a long chair at the club!

But little things like this didn't hinder our work, and soon we were able to say that we were ready. Biggs was ready, too. That is to say his name was attached to a finished script, but who was responsible for it in the end and which part had emanated from the brain of whom, it would have been very difficult to say. Anyhow it seemed quite good to us, and later on the papers were to call it the 'maddest, merriest potpourri of nonsense' ever heard in Singapore.

Happy days, those! I remember we used to finish the evenings with what one of the lads called a wassail bowl. I don't know what the concoction was, but think it consisted principally of beer. Anyhow it was harmless.

The nights up at the fort were beautifully cool, and the early mornings delightful. After a strenuous evening I used to sleep splendidly, except on those occasions when one or other of the fellows would take it into his head to go hunting in the roof. It was quite a common thing to be awakened by gunfire about two in the morning, only to find that one of the subs was having a little hunt all to himself.

One night I was awakened by something falling on my mosquito curtain. I got up, lit my lamp and discovered, to my

231

surprise, two legs hanging from the ceiling! Watson, I think it was, had gone hunting. Missing the rafters in the dark he had trodden on the ceiling boards, rotten with dry rot and white ants, and come through! Fortunately for him he had gone through on both sides of a rafter which supported him, otherwise he might have been seriously hurt.

Well, the great night arrived! All the wealth and beauty—and officialdom—of Singapore rolled up the hill in their carriages. They were accommodated in the auditorium of an excellent theatre, and for three hours we kept our audience—so the papers said at the time—'cackling and crowing with irresponsible merriment'. We called the play *Cinderella*, but it might just as well have been called *Hamlet* or *Il Trovatore* for all the clues the plot afforded. As a laughter-maker, though, it was immense. To quote the papers again:

'These people [the cast] between them made all the staid and responsible citizens of the town titter like so many blithering idiots for half the night, and for the other half they were shouting with laughter when they were not encoring.'

The dialogue spared no one. From the governor and General Dorward down to the Russian Baltic Squadron and the Tanjong Pagar deal, all were thrown into the pot to produce laughter. Even Piggy Burton's motorbike was roped in and made to produce the most horrible 'noises off'.

And I'm quite sure that none of the audience enjoyed it as much as we did. We had literally produced it. Scenery, play dresses, properties, even the very stage we strutted on had been made with our own hands, and we were extraordinarily proud of the result.

I have a very beautiful memento, in the shape of a valuable cigarette box, which was given to me after the show by the Fort Canning fellows as a mark of appreciation of my efforts. I value it very highly.

And what of all those cheery lads that worked and played together during those months at the end of 1904? Davidson, poor fellow, died in Kelantan, and the Abbotts I never heard of after they left here. Watson came back once to Singapore on leave from India; Piggy Burton I ran into at the Galle Face Hotel in Colombo and was greeted with: 'Good Lord, it's Brown. God bless you, have a drink.' Biggs, I think, was a colonel in Egypt during the war, and the others went their ways, ways which have not again crossed mine.

But we had good fun together.

One story about Biggs I must relate as it also gives an insight into the autocratic ways of old Buckley. It was at Christmas time, and Buckley was giving his usual Christmas parties to the children of Singapore. On these occasions a select party, headed by Mr and Mrs Salzmann, used to be present to sing Christmas carols. Biggs was, at that moment, languishing in the train of Nellie, Mrs Salzmann's daughter, and he begged Mrs Salzmann to smuggle him in with the party, though he couldn't sing a note. He was told to meet us at the Europe for an early dinner at half past six, and he duly arrived—in mess kit! What were we to do? There was no time to send him back to change and he couldn't get in by himself, so we decided to chance it.

Now there were big iron expanding gates at the town hall and Buckley, who usually did everything himself, used to stand there and take the tickets (issued by himself). When he had let a certain number through he used to shut and lock the gates, shepherd those who had come in upstairs, got them seated and amused, and then come down to the gates and let in another batch.

The way Mrs Salzmann worked things was this. She hid Biggs behind a pillar of the porch and then, just as Buckley was about to close the gates, appeared with her party. Buckley had to let us in, and she said: 'Now you go along upstairs, Brown will take the next batch of tickets till you come down again.' Buckley fell for it and departed. As soon as he had gone Biggs was let in and taken up onto the veranda. Hidden by Mrs Salzmann's ample skirts, he was safely brought to where the piano was in a corner. There he was told to sit down behind the piano and not to move or show himself on any account. Buckley relieved me at the gate in due course, and the enterprise—until then—had been carried safely through.

But disaster was to follow. Biggs began to feel a bit out of things. Even the pleasure of gazing upon a lady palls after a time, especially if one has to do the gazing from a low camp stool behind a piano. Speech, except an occasional whisper, was denied him and he could, of course, see nothing of what was going on in the hall. A great burst of laughter from the children was too much for him and, forgetting everything for the moment, he jumped up to see what the fun was. And at that precise moment Buckley turned and saw him! The games were stopped. The children stood in silence while Buckley, majestic in his wrath, descended upon poor Biggs. He took him by the collar, marched him the full length of the hall and down the stairs to the entrance gates where Biggs was cast out into the darkness and the gates locked behind him. Whether there was any wailing and gnashing of teeth at the time I cannot say. Afterwards, though, Biggs was highly amused at the whole thing, and rather prided himself on being the one man who had ever gate-crashed (though the word had not then been invented) on old Buckley!

And now the last incident of the year, and also the last one of any interest before I left on my first home leave.

It is about a tiger! And it is a very funny thing that these tigers always seemed to appear after some special occasion! This one visited the Chief Justice, Sir Lionel Cox, on the night of Boxing Day, 26 December, though it is said that the majesty of the law knew nothing about the incident until it was all over.

At about half past ten in the evening Police-Sergeant Reynolds, at Orchard Road police station, was visited by some excited Malays who said there was a tiger at Goodwood House. Being sceptical of the story, the sergeant nevertheless took a gun and some cartridges, and went with the men. Coming to Goodwood Hill more excited Malays met him, and he was assured of the presence of some beast or other.

He was led to the dwelling of the *kebun* (gardener), a hut standing off the ground about two feet under which was, or rather had been, a fowl roost, for now it contained only feathers to show its use. From among the feathers and fluff there came a growl, and it was certain that some animal had been doing damage and was still on the premises. Reynolds lay down and waited. Presently he saw eyes and, taking careful aim, fired. The growling ceased and quiet reigned. After a decent interval Reynolds crawled under the house to find that his shot had been successful, and that a fine specimen of what was known as the mottled tiger lay dead before him. It was small, measuring about six feet from tip to tip, and was judged by the naturalists to be about twelve years old.

And that, I think, was the last of the tigers. Though others were reported from time to time, I don't think any were actually bagged within what might be termed the Singapore residential area.

And with the passing of that tiger, I conclude these reminiscences of my first four years in Singapore.

Perhaps I shall be moved to continue them at some future time, who knows?

If you like this you'll like ...

If you enjoyed *Indiscreet Memories*, Monsoon Books has other similar titles which you'll be sure to want to read.

monsoon

If you like this, you'll
like...

If you've enjoyed reading this and want
to take a look at other similar titles,
simply visit The Reading Hut website:

www.thereadinghut.co.uk

SOLD FOR SILVER

An Autobiography of a Girl Sold into Slavery in Southeast Asia

Janet Lim

'I was looked at, criticized, and after much bargaining sold for $250.'

So begins Janet Lim's ordeal as a *mui tsai*, or slave girl, in 1930s Singapore. But this is only the beginning of a remarkable journey, which sees the author freed from child bondage to assume a position of leadership and obtain true happiness in later life.

After gaining her freedom, Janet is educated by missionaries and serves under colonial tutelage as a nurse. Her misfortunes return, however, when Singapore falls to the Japanese in 1942—the ship that she flees Singapore on is bombed and she drifts for days at sea. Rescued by Indonesian fishermen, she is finally captured and imprisoned in Japanese-occupied Sumatra. To avoid becoming a comfort woman, Janet escapes into the jungle villages of west Sumatra but is once again caught, and this time tortured by the Japanese military police and threatened with the firing squad.

ISBN: 978-981-05-1728-1

(Monsoon Books, 2004)

A COMPANY OF PLANTERS

Confessions of a Colonial
Rubber Planter in 1950s Malaya

John Dodd

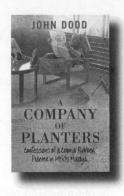

Through a collection of letters written to
his best friend and father in England, and
from his own personal diary entries, the young rubber planter
John Dodd has bequeathed us a fascinating, and often hilarious,
memoir of life as a colonial rubber planter.

With true stories and confessions that would make even
Somerset Maugham blush, we discover what life was really like
for young colonial planters in late-1950s Malaya. Life was more
than just a series of *stengahs* in the clubhouse, dalliances in the
Chinese brothels of Penang and charming 'pillow dictionaries'—
there were strikes, riots, snakes, plantation fires and deadly
ambushes by Communist terrorists to contend with. Set against
the backdrop of the Emergency period, the rise of nationalism
and Malaya's subsequent Independence, *A Company of Planters*
is a very personal, moving and humorous account of one man's
experiences on the frequently isolated rubber plantations of
colonial Malaya.

ISBN: 978-981-05-7569-4

(Monsoon Books, 2007)

YOU'LL DIE IN SINGAPORE

The True Account of One of the Most Amazing POW Escapes in WWII

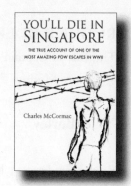

Charles McCormac

Weakened by hunger, thirst and ill-treatment, author Charles McCormac, then a WWII prisoner of war in Japanese-occupied Singapore, knew that if he did not escape he would die. With sixteen others he broke out of Pasir Panjang camp and began an epic two-thousand-mile escape from the island of Singapore, through the jungles of Indonesia to Australia.

With no compass and no map, and only the goodwill of villagers and their own wits to rely on, the British and Australian POWs' escape took a staggering five months and only two out of the original seventeen men survived.

You'll Die in Singapore is Charles McCormac's compelling true account of one of the most horrifying and amazing escapes in WWII. It is a story of courage, endurance and compassion, and makes for a very gripping read.

ISBN: 978-981-05-3015-0

(Monsoon Books, 2005)

ROGUE RAIDER
The Tale of Captain Lauterbach and the
Singapore Mutiny

Nigel Barley

Rogue Raider is a humorous fictionalised
history set in Singapore and Southeast Asia
during the First World War. The story centres on a lovable rogue
in the form of Captain Julius Lauterbach of the German Imperial
Navy and the ship that catapulted Lauterbach to accidental fame
(and infamy), His Imperial Majesty's *Emden*.

For every austere virtue of the *Emden*'s noble, ruthless and
gentlemanly commander Lieutenant-Commander Karl von
Mueller, it seems Lauterbach possessed the corresponding vice. He
was a beer-guzzling, cigar-smoking filcher, a braggart and, above
all, a survivor. The Flashmanesque Lauterbach was more interested
in making money, hoarding the spoils of war and womanising
than actually fighting in the war. Imprisoned in Singapore by the
British, he instigated the Singapore Mutiny among his Indian
guards as a diversion and made his escape. The book follows his
adventures and subsequent flight from the British through Asia to
America and back to Germany.

ISBN: 978-981-05-5949-6

(Monsoon Books, 2006)

THE FLIGHT OF THE SWANS

D. Devika Bai

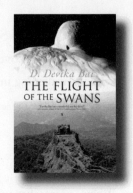

The Flight of the Swans is a rich and fascinating family saga set in British India and Malaya. Cursed, and with blood on his hands, Captain Ramdas Rao Bhonsle is forced to flee Killa Fort, which has fallen to the British. A strange flight of swans signals his flight from Killa; a flight that will drive Ramdas and his family into further adversity. But great adversity spawns great dreams. Ramdas dreams of ousting the British from his motherland. His sons dream of possessing the same girl, Tara Bai, the most beautiful courtesan in the land. And Ramdas' granddaughter, blind Arundhati, dreams only of seeing one day.

At once magical, poignant and exotic, Devika Bai's debut novel mesmerises as it unravels the love, loyalty and courage of the Bhonsles. The saga unfolds against the backdrop of war, famine, family conflict and social injustice, and hurtles towards its inevitable end in a masterful blend of history and fiction.

ISBN: 978-981-05-2367-1

(Monsoon Books, 2006)

THE ROSE OF SINGAPORE

An Epic Tale of Love, Loss and
Sexual Awakening in 1950s Malaya
and Singapore

Peter Neville

When Aircraftman First Class Peter
Saunders of the Royal Air Force leaves England for the Far East
in 1951, he is only eighteen years of age. His two-and-a-half-
year tour of duty takes him briefly to Hong Kong and Malaya
before being posted as a cook to RAF Changi, Singapore. For
an adventurous young man such as Peter, Singapore in the early
1950s holds all the promise of the Orient—exotic surroundings,
unusual customs and mesmerising women. Peter soon meets and
falls in love with a local Chinese girl but only later does he learn
she is not entirely what she seems.

The Rose of Singapore is a moving work of fiction about love,
loss and sexual awakening and is based on the true experiences of
the author, Peter Neville. The backdrop is Singapore and Malaya
during the Emergency period—a time of active Communist
terrorism as well as rising nationalism. Neville describes in minute
detail daily life at that time, bringing vividly to life the Singapore
and Malaya of old in this Tanamera-style blockbuster.

ISBN: 978-981-05-1727-4

(Monsoon Books, 2005)

THE RED THREAD

A Chinese Tale of Love and Fate in 1830s Singapore

Dawn Farnham

Like Chinese silk, *The Red Thread* is, by turns, gentle and strong, exploring a love that breaks through the divide of race and culture, a love that is both deeply physical and a marriage of souls.

Set against the backdrop of 1830s Singapore where piracy, crime, triads and tigers were commonplace, this romance follows the struggle of two lovers: Zhen, once the lowliest of Chinese coolies and triad member, later chosen to marry into a wealthy family of Chinese merchants, and Charlotte, a young Scots girl, sister of Singapore's Head of Police. Two souls bound together by the invisible threads of fate yet separated by bonds of tradition and culture.

By incorporating real figures from Singapore's historical past, Dawn Farnham brings to life the heady atmosphere of Old Singapore, where beliefs and customs clash and jostle in the struggle to make a life and create understanding between peoples from different worlds.

ISBN: 978-981-05-7567-0

(Monsoon Books, 2007)

THE BOAT

Singapore Escape

Cannibalism at Sea

Walter Gibson

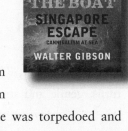

In 1942 a ship carrying 500 escapees from Japanese-occupied Singapore set sail from Padang for Ceylon. Halfway to safety she was torpedoed and sank. Amidst the horror and confusion, only one lifeboat was launched—a lifeboat built to carry twenty-eight but to which 135 souls now looked to for salvation.

For twenty-six days she drifted across the Indian Ocean. For twenty-six days, cannibalism, murder, heroism and self-sacrifice drifted with her. When the lifeboat finally ran aground on the island of Sipora, only four had survived: two Javanese seamen, a Chinese girl, Doris Lim, and Walter Gibson of the Argyll and Sutherland Highlanders.

The Boat is Walter Gibson's true account of that horrific event. He captures vividly the mental trauma, the physical pain, the decision to kill or be killed but above all, the determination not to die.

ISBN: 978-981-05-8301-9

(Monsoon Books, 2007)